WHAT A BLOODY ARRIVAL

A Wartime Story of Survival

WHAT A BLOODY ARRIVAL

A Wartime Story of Survival

Martin Smith

Compiled by Joanna Maynard

The Book Guild Ltd
Sussex, England

The Book Guild Ltd
25 High Street
Lewes, Sussex

First published 1997
© Martin Smith 1997
Set in Times
Typesetting by Poole Typesetting (Wessex) Ltd, Bournemouth
Printed in Great Britain by
Antony Rowe Ltd, Chippenham, Wiltshire

A catalogue record for this book is available
from the British Library

ISBN 1 85776 174 X

FOREWORD

What a Bloody Arrival is about the life of Martin Smith – Lincolnshire farmer, wartime RAF pilot, husband, father and grandfather. The majority of the book, however, focuses on his remarkable first-hand perspective of the air war over European coastal waters from Brittany to Norway, and on Martin's unorthodox arrival on a small Norwegian island in July 1942.

I first met Martin in 1982 when I moved with my family to the small village of Greatford in south Lincolnshire. Although I knew of him as a retired farmer who had lived in the village for many years, I soon realised that there had been another side to his life. At the Service of Remembrance held in the village church each year, Martin always calls out the names of the men from Greatford who lost their lives in the service of their country. At the first such service we attended, a few months after moving into the village, I noticed that Martin wore the Distinguished Flying Medal.

However, I didn't learn anything of his exploits for 12 years. Then, I discovered that Martin had been a wartime Blenheim and Beaufighter pilot operating over the waters between Brittany and Norway. His flying career had been cut short in July 1942 when he had ditched his Beaufighter 30 miles off the Norwegian coast. He and his navigator had drifted in their rubber dinghy (without drinking water or food) for three days until they were eventually washed up on a small island. They were taken in by a Norwegian farmer and his family, but the Germans came the next day to take them away. They spent the rest of the war in a prison camp.

When Martin wrote this book – so that his grandchildren would know something of his life – he found that the task could not be completed until he had returned to Norway to find out for himself what had happened to those who had given shelter to his navigator and himself. He asked me to help him identify the island and to see if I could trace those who had helped him. There began a fascinating few months of research. In due course we became reasonably certain that the island was Hindoy, near Askvoll in western Norway. Furthermore, we were able to identify two elderly women who had played a part in Martin's arrival on Hindoy 53 years previously. However, we could not be certain about the facts until Martin revisited the island.

During the spring of 1995, I drew up a rough schedule for Martin's visit to Norway which was planned to take place over the weekend of the 50th Anniversary of VE Day. As the details of the visit were firmed up during the following weeks, I became increasingly involved in its implementation, and Martin invited me to accompany him to Norway. We spent a memorable five days in Norway. Although it was an emotional visit for Martin and moving for us all, it was also great fun and the lasting impression is of the enormous warmth and friendliness of the Norwegian people and the intense interest they took in Martin and his exploits. It was certainly a weekend to cherish and remember, and it was a privilege to have been there.

Group Captain C. Granville-White CBE RAF

ACKNOWLEDGEMENT

I would like to thank the following people, all of whom have helped me in various ways with the preparation of this book:

Steve Bond, for his research into wartime records of 248 Squadron RAF
Peter Crew
Wing Commander Christopher Harper commanding officer of 41 Squadron
Major General Ejil Omdal and Lieutenant Colonel Helge Sandnes of the Royal Norwegian Air Force
The Mayoress of Askvoll, Mrs Kjellaug Hoyvik
Paal Fennell
Alfred Vorland
Jorgen Stang

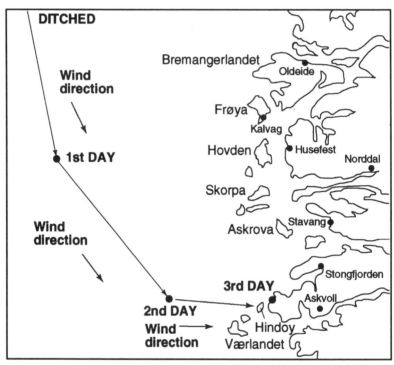

July 1942. Having been forced to ditch their Beaufighter, Martin and his navigator spent three days drifting in a dinghy off the coast of Norway.

1

My earliest recollection of aircraft is when I was six years old, fishing for dogfish off Hunstanton pier with my father and Jack Thurlby. An RAF biplane, travelling at about 1,000 feet roared over our heads, went into a spin and crashed into the sea not more than 200 yards from our little rowing boat. I watched the plane meet its watery grave with the round-eyed wonder of a small boy, never imagining that in 18 years' time I would watch my own aircraft disappear in exactly the same way.

Jack hurriedly raised anchor and Father rowed with all his might to the spot where we'd seen the plane disappear. Peering over the side of the boat, I was aghast at the paucity of remains of that magnificent machine – a scattering of misshapen debris bobbing on a small oil slick.

The eerie silence hanging over the scene was broken by the roar of motor boats arriving from Hunstanton. Father was advised to return to shore, the recovery of the pilot being considered no sight for a small child. As it was, recovery efforts proved futile and it was only at low tide that the sea relinquished its hold on the unfortunate airman, still strapped in his cockpit.

My second encounter with aircraft was no less dramatic and occurred only a matter of months after our fishing trip. We lived in the village of Castor in Cambridgeshire and I was happily playing in the farmyard one afternoon when I heard the sound of approaching aircraft. Glancing up I saw RAF biplanes in loose formation. The last plane was descending rapidly, smoke pouring from its engine. I was unable to move as I watched the string bag skim across the village, only a few feet from the highest roofs. The resounding crash on impact sent me running to the barn for my bike and I pedalled furiously through the village to a field just beyond the church.

Father's car was parked by the field gate and I was astonished to see him standing some 50 yards from the burning wreckage talking to the pilot. The remaining biplanes circled overhead for a time and then disappeared from view. My father and the pilot, who was uninjured, drove back to the farmhouse for a drink, having given me a stern warning to stay away from the wreckage.

The next day an officer arrived with a recovery crew and lorry. He asked my father if he would care for a piece of the aircraft as a momento, an offer which to my horror my father declined. Plucking up every shred of courage I announced that I would very much like a souvenir. I held my breath as the officer walked over to the tangled wreckage and picked out a piece of the burnt wooden airframe, measuring about nine square inches. He presented this to me, smiling at my obvious delight.

I treasured this souvenir for many years, intrigued by its smell of dope, varnish and burnt wood. It was only when in my early teens, short of cash as usual, I hocked my Hornby train set, a tin of old coins I had gathered from the old Roman road, Ermine Street, which ran through the farm, and my beloved piece of aircraft. I do not even recall what I received in exchange but something tells me mine was the poorer deal!

My fascination with aircraft continued and I well remember the excitement I felt when at the age of ten or eleven Mr Mathews, a wealthy businessman living in the next village, asked Father if friends of his, coming to stay for a weekend houseparty, could land their private aircraft in one of our meadows. The cattle were moved into an adjacent field and I eagerly offered to cut down all the jack thistles. This was a long and painstaking occupation but was not undertaken on my part without some idea of reward. I was convinced that the gratitude of these eminent people would result in them offering me a chance to fly in their plane.

I hung around the aeroplane most of the weekend and was careful to be there early on the Monday morning. Mindful of my

2

father's wrath should he hear of my actions, I quietly informed the pilot on his arrival of my good deed. He was most courteous in his thanks, indeed to the extent that he pressed four boiled sweets into my hand. Obviously if I was going to fly, I would have to try other means!

Schooldays were far from my happiest with my education typical of that of the farming community in the twenties. It was not considered the done thing for me to attend the local village school and so my first few years were spent with a Governess at home. I learnt very little from the succession of women who filled this role and thus equipped was sent as a border to Stamford School at the tender age of seven. From my arrival I spent most of my time in the bottom quarter of the class and it seemed little short of a miracle when I scraped through my school certificate at 17 and was able to leave. My horror on arriving at school was brought to a head three weeks into my first term when there was a half day holiday. My housemaster decided that I was too young to be allowed into town and that I must stay on my own in school. This irked me terribly and I decided that the next morning I would run away. I carefully planned my escape and my hideout.

Our farm was ten miles from the school and I knew that if I could get there I could go and live in the hollow willow tree I often played in. This was in a spinney about quarter of a mile from the village. Food would be easily obtainable from the village shop, money being no problem as I would charge everything to my mother's account.

The following morning I went to the locker room, put on my running shoes and set off for the A1. I reckoned that I had a good half an hour to get well clear of Stamford before role-call and prayers, when my absence would be discovered. I had only one near miss as I headed out of town. Walking alongside Burghley Park, I was met head on by a crocodile of Stamford High School girls on their morning walk. I realised with horror that my sister, Rachel would be amongst the group. Putting my head down, I sprinted past as fast as I could. Just as I reached the line's end I heard Rachel's voice call to the accompanying mistress, 'Miss Rhodes, that was my brother.' For a ghastly moment I thought I was to be pursued by a pack of schoolgirls but a hasty glance over my shoulder confirmed they were continuing sedately on their way.

I was almost seven miles into my journey when a bullnose Morris pulled up beside me and a gentleman in a clerical collar offered me a lift. I gratefully scrambled in, amazed at my good fortune and it was only as the car circled and headed back to Stamford that I recognised this good samaritan as my headmaster. Not a word was spoken until we reached the school and he led me into assembly. The whole school had been kept in the hall until I could be found and my embarrassment was indescribable as the Head delivered a short lecture on the seriousness of my antics. The dreaded cane was produced and I was given four of the best, my sole comfort being that I had expected six.

Needless to say my friends were pretty few and far between for the next few days and it was only my housemaster, Mr Evans and his wife who took pity on such an unfortunate little boy, even inviting me to tea the following Sunday. However unintentional, I had certainly made my mark and was branded 'The Runaway' for the rest of my schooldays.

This notoriety led to various other scrapes. I well remember a fight I had with another new boy soon after my bid for freedom. Cheered on by older boys, my opponent and I slogged out our differences for a good 20 minutes, finally interrupted by the prayer bell. As so often happens with schoolboys, my deadly foe soon after became a great friend and we would spend holidays together, a good lesson in learning to forgive and forget.

My passion for flying did not diminish. On half day holidays I would walk out to Wittering where the Central Flying School was based and spend cramped but enjoyable hours hiding in the hedges on the perimeter of the airfield. From this vantage point the aircraft were either taking off or landing right over my head. In my teens I also sought to take advantage of my sister Bridget's friendship with Verena Leach. Wing Commander Leach was Chief Flying Instructor at the Central Flying School and I always hoped that Verena might introduce me to her father who would of course then offer me a flight! Unfortunately for me Verena was a pretty and vivacious girl with plenty of admirers in her own right and I stood little chance of gaining any additional favours from her.

As it was my endeavours were suddenly ended when the Central Flying School moved to Upavon. Some years later, at the end of

4

the War, Verena married Paddy Bathrop who served with distinction in the Battle of Britain and incidentally was in the same compound as myself in Stalag Luft III.

Visiting air circuses were a major attraction for me and I would save desperately for weeks beforehand to be able to afford a flight. I was much helped in my endeavours by my Great Aunt Min who lived in Nottingham. Never dreaming to go in an aircraft herself, she viewed it as a most exciting venture and would ask me to stay when any shows were in her locality, more than enthusiastically buying me flights. With her help I was able to be a passenger in various stunt displays. The thrill of being airborne was intoxicating for me and I felt no fear as the pilots performed their antics.

My favourite stunt was one I took part in in a Gypsy Spartan. It involved the aircraft ascending to 1,500 feet from where toilet rolls were hurled out of the cockpit. The pilot then attempted to cut the paper into fragments using the propeller of the aircraft as his knife. The aim was to scatter the paper before any reached the ground. I know that the last strip was only six feet from the deck when it was cut. On another occasion I went aboard a Leopard Moth on a height-guessing trip. This was taken courtesy of Great Aunt Min who, ever eager that young people should have the chance to fly, also paid for her chauffeur to accompany me. The fact that this chauffeur was female, 20 years old and a glorious redhead to boot, seemed to have rather an impact on the pilot. Having courteously helped the girl into the small cabin in front of the cockpit, he carefully explained that he would be flying to 7,000 feet for the sake of the competition. No mention was made of the descent however which turned out to involve just about every stunt in the book, from tight rolls to steep turns.

At shows where Great Aunt Min was not available to subsidise me, and my savings amounted to very little, I would have to pick the very cheapest flights on offer. At one such event I handed over the princely sum of four shillings for the privilege of riding in a World War One aircraft with a landing skid. On climbing into the old war bus, I was given strict instructions not to put my head out of the cockpit as hot oil was continually being blown back from the engine. Coupled with the terrific vibration and noise during the flight, this was certainly one of my most unpleasant flying

5

experiences, and instilled in me a great respect for the brave pilots of the First World War.

As it came time for me to leave school I desperately hoped to go to Cranwell and take a permanent commission. Unfortunately opposition came from both my headmaster and my father. Canon Day (Gaffer John) was the epitome of the autocratic headmaster. Never one to spare the rod, boys were only acceptable if they were first and foremost good at cricket, and secondly likely fodder for Oxbridge. Medicine and teaching were his idea of a good career. Having initially disgraced myself by running away and compounded this by my regular position in the bottom quarter of the class, my final sin was an ineptitude at cricket. When I approached him with the idea of my trying for Cranwell it was immediately dismissed.

Undeterred, I voiced the idea of taking a short service commission with four years active service and then six years on the Reserve. These commissions were being offered in 1934 to those with the school certificate on satisfactory acceptance by the selection board. This time my father added his opposition. With no history of service in the family, he could not envisage what I would do when the four year term was up. As it happened, very few short service officers were ever discharged as the RAF Emergency Expansion Programme granted them permanent commissions. However my father's opposition was heightened when two of my friends, accepted for short service commissions, failed flying.

2

Even my father however realised the impracticality of me joining him on the farm. The depression of the twenties was still evident in agriculture and when I left school in 1935, not one of my fellow schoolmates from farming stock went on the land. For my part, I had no desire to farm. I had spent every summer from the age of ten helping with the harvest, long days spent walking with the shire horses from field to farmyard and back. Each year I would begin my toils with the promise of reward, but the story remained the same. The grain did not make a profit and nor did I, not so much as a trip to the pictures.

I certainly had no desire to be permanently employed in such a depressed industry and with my hopes of joining the RAF so firmly quashed, I sought around for an alternative career. It seemed to me that while farmers suffered, the middleman and merchant still made a good living out of agriculture. Jobs of any sort were not easy to come by at this time but I was lucky enough to have an uncle who put in a good word for me with a firm selling vegetables in Spitalfields market in London. Farmers sons were not the favourite employees of such companies as they had a tendency to learn the trade and then set up in competition with their own connections. However, as a favour to my uncle, I was hired as a general dogsbody, doing anything from fetching the tea and toast to adding up tedious columns of figures. I was excited at the prospect of living in London and was determined to make the most of life there, even on ten shillings a week!

At the end of my first week I had a meeting with the manager of the London company, Mr Treadwell, and was surprised to see he sported an Old Stamfordian tie. Too much the new boy to comment, I made sure that I wore mine the next time we met. This was the start of a long and happy friendship, culminating in our starting our own company after the war. Although some 15 years my senior, both Wilfred and his wife, Eileen made sure that I was not lonely during my time in London. I was particularly grateful for an introduction to Blackheath Rugby Club, Wilfred's brother being a vice-president, and I spent many cold winter Saturdays in a red and black jersey.

My hours of work were far from social. I had to be up at 3 a.m. to catch the market train from my digs in Catford through to London Bridge. This was followed by a 20 minute walk to the market enabling me to arrive for the 4.30 a.m. start. Surprisingly, this walk was one of my favourite parts of the day. London was only just waking as I set off across London Bridge, my only companions the odd taxi and the fast clip-clop of the costers pony carts. I would look down at the Thames and see ships being loaded and unloaded by the lights of the warehouses, before the pungent smell of fresh fish would herald my arrival at Billingsgate market. Leadenhall meat market followed quickly on and I would pass through an avenue being hung with red carcasses before arriving amid the greenery of Spitalfield. The earthy aroma of caulis and potatoes was balanced by the sweet scent of boxes of citrus fruits newly arrived from exotic locations.

I witnessed London waking when a mantle of white December snow covered the ships and turned the Thames as grey as granite and when the mid-June sunrise burnt crimson on the water. For me this was the City in all her glory. I had somewhat less romantic emotions about the journey home. If I was lucky the day would finish at 4 p.m., but that was only if the stock and cash balanced correctly. I would often find myself willing the last greengrocer home for there was no such luxury as paid overtime. On occasions I would still be at the market at 7 p.m.. My long hours were rewarded with promotion however, and over the next two years I became cashier and finally salesman with a salary of £6 per week.

This was no mean income for a 19-year-old and I began to think I was well on the way to a good career.

Market life greatly broadened my horizons. The cast of traders ranged from the East End Cockney with his pony and cart, the street stallholder in Hackney, Poplar or Deptford, the Whitechapel Jews and the high class fruiterers and greengrocers with shops on high streets throughout London. All enjoyed dealing in different ways and all drove a hard bargain, especially the Cockney. Naturally abrasive, I had to learn quickly to give as good as I got when dealing with these people. At the same time I developed a great liking for them. Ruthless in business, I witnessed many occasions when a Cockney would give his all in helping someone in a time of need.

3

The Munich Crisis in September 1938 sent an uneasy shudder through my secure world. I fervently agreed with Chamberlain and hoped for peace in our time, but over the next six months as Hitler and Mussolini continued to gain power I realised that war was inevitable.

At the beginning of August 1939, I withdrew every last penny from my bank account and went on holiday to Torquay with two friends. By the end of the week we were broke and exhausted, having had a tremendous time. Although we spoke about it very little, the shadow of war hung over us and in our hearts we knew it could be a long time before we would holiday again.

On our return, a more pressing cloud covered my horizon. A letter from my bank manager informed me that I was over-drawn by 2/6d and must attend a meeting at the bank the next day. My father who had stood guarantor for the account had also been notified and had to be present. My father's fury at my incompetence was increased by the fact that he had to cancel a day at Huntingdon races to come up to London. I met him at King's Cross Station and suffered the full force of his scorn on our journey to the Westminster bank in Spitalfields. Neither did the bank manager spare my feelings, expressing astonishment that I had not raised an overdraft facility to cover this error.

My teenage ego took a little while to recover from these charges of stupidity, my great consolation being that it was a lesson that stood me in good stead for the rest of my life. I returned to work determined to impress the bank manager and rebuild my account, blissfully unaware how short the time to do so would be.

Three weeks later, on the morning of 1 September, I was busily tucking into a plate of bacon and eggs in a market café, when the news of Germany's invasion of Poland came over the wireless. For a few seconds the noisy chatter of the traders was stilled as everyone absorbed the implication of this bulletin. Amid the outcry that immediately followed, I realised that I no longer felt hungry. Leaving my half finished breakfast I walked out into the market. My mind was already made up, I would join up that afternoon.

Like everyone else who had listened to the recent propaganda, I was very optimistic about our chances should Hitler's threats turn to war. I quite believed that our fighter squadrons were fully operational with Spitfires and Hurricanes at the ready. The Blenheim was far superior to any German medium bomber and, so we'd been told, the lumbering Whitley could break through any defences. The Navy for its part was quite invincible, supported by the very latest high-tech equipment and of course the Army had any number of secret weapons at its disposal. Indeed I had overheard Uncle Cyril telling Father about a secret weapon which he had happened upon while touring with Aunt Margaret. Approaching the picturesque town of Southwold on the Suffolk coast, the engine of Uncle Cyril's beloved Rolls Royce had suddenly gone dead. A mechanic had been called out and simply by adjusting the distributor had restarted the engine. When Uncle Cyril expressed concern over the problem returning, the mechanic gave him a knowing smile and in a hushed voice explained the reason for the fault. The Army, he said, were testing a laser beam capable of immobilising an engine within a radius of several miles. It was designed to be one of the most powerful war weapons available. In the meantime, he was constantly being called out to deal with the electrics on cars caught by the beam.

Armed with such stories, I felt totally confident when at 5 p.m. that day I arrived at Adastral House. The foyer was packed with people all eager to join up. I eventually managed to see a sergeant who told me that the only available positions were for short service commissions. By this time I was determined to enrol in whatever capacity I could find and I filled out the forms

11

immediately while the sergeant explained that in the event of war breaking out before my application had been processed, it would become void and I would have to enrol as an AC 2 at a recruitment centre. The feeling of comradeship that I was to come to treasure, was evident even at this early stage. I soon got talking to a group of similar aged men and we adjourned to a nearby pub for a few beers. We were alight with a combination of trepidation and excitement.

Early the next morning I took the train to Peterborough to spend the weekend with my family at Thorney where my father was now farming. King's Cross Station was in turmoil with evacuees leaving and the hasty erection of sandbag defences blocking passenger walkways. I was not particularly good company for any of my family that weekend, being preoccupied with the feeling of a vast change in my life. The possibility of war was a constant subject but I remained silent about my visit to Adastral House, unwilling to upset my mother. On Sunday, the outbreak of war was declared and I knew that the next day I would volunteer.

Arriving back in London I contacted the Air Ministry and found that the nearest recruiting station had been hastily housed in a large pub at Eltham, south-east London. Leaving work early on the Monday I arrived at the pub at 3 p.m. and found that the queue to join up with the RAF was a hundred yards long. Those wishing to join the Navy had a ten-yard wait while recruits for the Army could go straight in. Seven hours later I was finally enlisted and told to report back in two days time with an extra two pairs of socks.

My notice at work was duly handed in on the Tuesday. Everybody fully understood and wished me the best of luck. Reporting back on the Wednesday I found about a hundred men present. We were all sent to Uxbridge to be given the shilling and kitted out. Uniforms were somewhat ad hoc with late arrivals receiving old high collar tunics from the First World War. At the end of the day we spent the first night of many under canvas. The next two days were spent waiting to go before the Selection Board. This was the same board as for short service commissions in peacetime, comprising three Group Captains and back-up staff.

The application forms gave three options to be put in order of choice, pilot, airgunner and observer. I was so determined to be a pilot that I was amazed at the number of people opting for the latter two positions. However, it soon became obvious from the men emerging from their interview that the board were looking for airgunners and observers. When my interview finally came, I stood nervously in front of the gold braid while I was delivered a short lecture in the importance of being an observer. The pilot, I was told, was little short of a bus driver and this would be reflected by the fact observers would be made Captains before pilots were. My heart sunk as I realised that I was destined to be an observer, when suddenly one of the Group Captains noticed that under the sports section I had put that I rode and hunted. Having remarked on this to his fellow board members, it was agreed that I could embark on pilot training.

Filled with delight I inwardly thanked my sisters for the use of their ponies which I had ridden and hunted in school holidays. Strangely this was not the last time I heard an instructor compare flying an aircraft to riding a horse. Both aircraft and horses can be temperamental and require gentle handling. To overcorrect a horse is as disastrous as overcorrecting an aircraft. Above all, both flying and riding demand total concentration. Indeed when the RAF was initially formed, the first members were drawn from cavalry regiments.

About 60 of the group of 100 I'd arrived at Uxbridge with were taken on as aircrew after the interview, but now we all faced the medical. This was still the peacetime standard medical and waiting in the ante-room to be seen by the various medical officers, we all admitted our main worry was the mercury test. This involved blowing mercury up a U-tube and holding it at 40-pound pressure for a minute. In the event, I found holding my breath for 90 seconds the main horror. After a minute I just wanted to rip the nose clasp off, but somehow I hung on for those last vital seconds. The medical failures were chiefly through colour-blindness. Eyesight and hearing had to be excellent and for many it was a shock to find they were below par. At the end of the medicals we had lost about 20 per cent of our intake.

I remember the evening after the medicals the film *Dawn Patrol* was showing at the camp cinema. Set in the First World War there were scenes where whole squadrons were wiped out and only the hero, Errol Flynn, survived. Later in the NAAFI we joked about the film, all confident that no such destruction would occur in this war. How little we knew.

On the fifth day, all those accepted for training were given a fortnight's pay of 28 shillings and sent on indefinite leave. We were instructed to buy books on a variety of topics, including advanced mathematics, trigonometry and mechanics. Needless to say my head reeled at the thought of the dreaded studying which came even harder four years out of school. I purchased the required material however and set off for home, expecting along with everyone else to be back in a couple of weeks.

4

Our recall did not come until the first week of January. No living allowance had been paid and for some men who had given up their jobs to join up, life was very tough. I was lucky as I worked on the farm, but even so life was frustrating. Each day I would expect a letter telling me to return to London and it was difficult to concentrate on everyday matters when I was so keyed up about what lay ahead.

When at last I returned to Uxbridge the group was divided into two, half going to Hastings Initial Training Wing and the rest of us to Cambridge Initial Training Wing. At Cambridge we were billeted in the colleges, two men to share a bedroom and a sitting room. The town was swamped with RAFVR who were all officers and sergeants. We had a high proportion of university students, many of whom had interrupted their degrees to join up. It was nothing to see AC 2s driving around in Bentleys or Aston Martins. Regardless of our former position in life, we were all made Leading Aircraftmen and received 17 shillings a week. We wore white bands around our caps to show that we were trainees.

The course lasted for eight weeks and consisted of lectures on theory of flight navigation, mathematics and gunnery slotted around hours of square bashing. I soldiered on as best I could with the academic side but was easily distracted. The first two months of 1940 were bitterly cold and there was excellent skating on the flooded meadows just outside the town. Always a keen skater I had my boots sent from home and spent many hours charging after a wooden puck in frantic games of ice hockey. As these games frequently ate into what should have been my study time, I consoled my guilty conscience with the fact that skating kept me supremely fit.

At the end of the two months training, we sat a series of exams. I was fortunate to count among my friends two or three university chaps who positioned themselves in front, at the side and behind me during the exams, in case I floundered and needed help. As it happened I did not require their help and was delighted to pass on my own merit. Earlier on in the course we had all had a week's training on the link trainer and I had been graded above average. Together with my exam pass this gave me great confidence for my future flying training. My eagerness to progress though was somewhat thwarted by bureaucracy. The RAF flying training programme was still trying to gear itself up to a wartime footing and coupled with this, the severe winter had curtailed flying at all training stations creating a logjam of pilots waiting for postings. By the end of March there were still pilots of the Voluntary Reserves at the Initial Training Wings waiting for postings to Elementary Flying Training Schools.

Having finished our exams we were caught in this hold-up and were forced to fill our days with long route marches and endless square bashing. The main relief was that as the worst frost left the ground we were able to play rugby. I was in the wing's second team and enjoyed a number of matches against Cambridgeshire operational aerodomes. This was the time of the phoney war, so the bomber stations could still field some good teams. The phoney war was so named because after the declaration of war in September 1939 there was almost a lull until the following spring.

We also maintained a fairly gruelling nightlife and I soon got to know every pub in Cambridge and the surrounding area. We were particularly fond of pubs with a piano as within our group we had the organist from the Empire, Leicester Square, Jack Sabren. He really could make the ivories jump and I remember some terrific nights with Jack at the keyboard. Sadly, I believe he was reported missing in 1941.

By the end of April these high jinks could no longer hide the frustration we were all feeling at the delays, so we were sent on a fortnight's leave. I went back to Thorney feeling somewhat deflated. It was now seven months since I had joined up and I was no further than my initial training. The urgency of the previous September seemed a lifetime away.

At the beginning of the second week of leave, Germany invaded the low countries and we were immediately recalled. I arrived back at Cambridge with high hopes that flying training was imminent. Indeed within two days rumour had it that we were going to be posted to operational stations and taught to fly in Avro Tudors, Tiger Moths and Magisters, which at that time were kept for the station masters and pilots to use for pleasure. This rumour was purposely leaked by the Orderly Room, the truth being that we were being posted as ground defence. Had we found this out beforehand, I am quite sure there would have been a mutiny. I understand that the Hastings group did discover it was a con and created a serious uproar. We were divided into groups of eight according to the alphabetical role call lists and sent on our way. My group, containing five people with the surname Smith, was destined for Dishforth in Yorkshire.

On arrival we were greeted by a boorish regular flight sergeant who ordered us to take off our white cap flashes immediately and to report that night to man eight Lewis guns placed at intervals around the airfield's perimeter. The next six weeks were some of the most frustrating and unhappy days of my whole RAF career. The flight sergeant's dislike of us as volunteer aircrew was evident and his temper was shortened further by having five Smiths among an intake of eight new recruits. Both he and the Orderly Room were constantly muddling us up and the five Smiths did everything possible to increase the confusion. The eight of us were assigned to different barrack rooms and were somewhat ostracised by the other AC 2s who were ground staff as opposed to aircrew. I certainly missed the camaraderie of the Cambridge group.

After about three weeks I managed to obtain a 24-hour pass and set out for Leeds, confident that I would meet up with a group I could share a night out with. Unfortunately it was a night shortly after the evacuation of France via Dunkirk and I'd barely ordered my first pint before I was tackled by two army privates about the lack of support given by the RAF. I quickly moved on to another pub, only to find this one also full of army privates claiming to have been evacuated from Dunkirk. It was certainly not a night to be a lone airman in Leeds. Everywhere I went I encountered the anger and ridicule of the Army concerning the RAF's inadequacy at Dunkirk. This bitterness actually lasted the whole summer until the RAF was able to scotch the remarks with the Battle of Britain in September.

By the time I returned to camp the next day, my morale was at a very low ebb. The media was full of the heroics of the Army and of their current regrouping for the future. Reading the papers I began to think that if I was to see any action at all I would have to transfer to the Army. Much as I yearned to fly, I really thought the war would be over by the time I made the grade. With a heavy heart I went to see the Station Warrant Officer to request a transfer. My luck was in that day for the chap I saw was a World War One veteran and not one of the normal paper pushers. He told me that he could not refuse my request but that in his opinion I was making a big mistake and that pilots would desperately be needed before the end of the war. I left his office feeling far more optimistic than I had for weeks, confident that this period of ground defence would soon be over.

A fortnight later our individual postings arrived and I set off for White Waltham in Berkshire. White Waltham was a civilian flying school owned by De Haviland. It was a showpiece, immaculately kept with even the mechanics in spotless white overalls emblazoned with the company logo. We slept in barrack rooms, cleaned each day by an army of civilian cleaners and were fed by a civilian catering company, devouring some of the best meals I ever tasted in the RAF. There was no ante-room which gave us a good excuse for nights out in Maidenhead and as we were now receiving flight pay this helped out considerably for beers. The civilian flying instructors had all been commissioned into the RAF and we had an RAF station CO. I was assigned to an ex-Oxford University air squadron instructor, Flying Officer Kemp, who I immediately took a liking to and I eagerly awaited my first familiarising flight, scheduled for 1400 hours on the first Sunday after our arrival.

On the day, I got to the field 15 minutes early and stood admiring the sight of the Tiger Moths. There were five rows of aircraft with nine in each row, all wing tip to wing tip in front of the watch tower.

I was reminded of peacetime Sunday rallies and felt exhilarated at the thought that at last I was to receive flight instruction. I walked across to the parachute store beside the watch tower and was just taking a chute out when all hell broke lose. I remember being thrown against a wall as the world seemed to explode around me. I staggered to my feet, brushing off splinters of glass and chunks of plaster and ran outside to a scene of total devastation. About 20 of the Tiger Moths had been blown to pieces and fire raged through them. I joined people running across the field and we began to push clear the aircraft that weren't burning. A sudden shout sent us diving for cover as our attacker, a Heinkel 111 was spotted lining up for another run. It was travelling at about 1,500 feet with 7/10 cloud cover, just hopping from cloud to cloud. This time it targeted the hangars causing terrific damage and five casualties.

With no time to lose, the rest of the Tiger Moths had to be dispersed. The CO ordered every available pupil to taxi the remaining aircraft to the far edges of the field. Somehow I didn't feel this was a good time to tell him that I had never even been in a Tiger cockpit. I climbed up into the aircraft and wondered what the civilian mechanic swinging the prop would think if he knew I was a complete novice. On the third swing the engine spluttered into life and I headed across the field just as fast as everybody else although in a decidedly more erratic fashion. By late afternoon all the Tiger Moths had been dispersed into three large fields in the locality.

We had certainly been caught unawares in one of the first attacks on airfields in Southern England. It was a good few minutes after the second attack that the air raid siren went off and at least five minutes later before a lone Hurricane circled the airfield. White Waltham had been reluctant to alter its image of a peaceful weekend flying school and there had been no defence, not even a Lewis gun. Not surprisingly, this episode brought home to me with full force the reality of war. It certainly subdued the boyish enthusiasm of many of us and I think there was a greater effort put into training by everyone.

When we were eventually able to fly we completed two hours circuit flying and landing before being moved to the satellite fields for further training. Our flight shared a 35-acre field with a herd of

Fresian cows and we had to work our flying time to coincide with their milking. We had a roster for 'tenting' the cows, but if they moved too far from one end of the field, an instructor would do some cattle driving with a Tiger Moth. This manoeuvre was stopped when one of the instructors, with a pupil on board, clipped the ground with a wing, somersaulting the aircraft four times before it landed on its back. It was a truly spectacular crash and both men were extremely lucky to survive. The pupil, who was a friend of mine, was struggling to go solo and managed to persuade the Chief Flying Instructor for another two hours following the disaster which was not his fault. I was sad to find that he still didn't achieve his goal.

During this part of our training we all lived very much from day to day aware that if we messed up there were no second chances. It was not unusual for a recruit to return from a session with his instructor and be told to pack his bags. Understandably the RAF did not want to waste money and time training those of low aptitude and I witnessed some extremely tough chaps very close to tears when they were rejected.

If you hadn't gone solo after 12 hours flying you were out. Luckily I didn't have long to wait. Coming up to my six and a quarter hours, I completed my training one day with four perfect daisy cutting landings. I secretly put this down to a severe hangover and the cricket pitch conditions of White Waltham, but my instructor was suitably impressed and told me I could go solo. I still recall the jubilation I felt at this news. Flying failures were about 20 per cent at this stage and I certainly did not wish to be among them.

Along with the training failures there were also training tragedies. While at White Waltham I bunked next to a young chap who was very reserved. I would always ask him along on nights when a crowd of us was going out, but he never accepted. Halfway through his flight training his aircraft plummeted out of the sky tail first, killing both himself and his instructor. I was ordered to attend the enquiry and gave what little information I had about him, mainly that he was a complete loner. Combined with their own facts, the enquiry came to the conclusion that the student simply froze at the controls. I was quite shocked to hear this as up until then I had considered freezing at the controls was a myth and simply not possible.

There was great excitement midway through the course when a number of aircraft were called in for maintenance and reappeared with bomb racks to carry four 20 pound bombs. For the next few evenings the instructors practiced dive-bombings over neighbouring fields. The rumour went round that in the event of an invasion and there not being sufficient instructors to fly the Tiger Moths, then the students would have to do so. As on so many other occasions this eventuality never happened and for my part I was most glad. Tiger Moths dive-bombing at 100 m.p.h. looked incredibly pathetic.

As the time for my passing-out test loomed I found myself increasingly worried about my ability to roll the aircraft. I owed a lot to my instructor's patience but even he despaired of my performance in this manoeuvre. Try as I would I could not seem to maintain the speed. I well remember my feeling of horror during the test when at 2,000 feet the Chief Flying Instructor ordered me to roll. Knowing that this height was no safety margin for my rolls I laboriously began to climb to 4,000 feet. After a few minutes his irritated voice came over the speaking tube demanding to know what I was doing. Aware of the black points I was amassing I threw caution to the wind and with the altimeter reading 3,200 feet went into a roll. Sure enough it was a total disaster, dropping 900 feet. My passenger's only comment was that he could see why I was trying to get to gain height.

In spite of this incident I passed my flying test and somehow struggled through my written exams. Half of each day was taken up with lectures on navigational mathematics, met and theory of flight. Throughout the course I had battled manfully with these subjects but must admit that I was grateful to friends who once again grouped round me in the exam room and whose help I utilised this time. We held our farewall party at Skindles in Maidenhead. Skindles was actually for officers only but as all our instructors were commissioned they let us have a back room. It was a night to remember, partly, obviously, because of the antics and alcohol, but I think we also felt that we had overcome a major hurdle in passing our flying and were justifiably proud of ourselves.

5

At this stage we were given the option to fly single or twin-engine aircraft. I was definite that I wanted to fly twin. As far as I could see if you had two engines you had a chance if one packed up and besides my aerobatics were not good enough for fighters. Having made this decision I found myself posted to Shawbury in Shropshire with four others from White Waltham.

We arrived on a Saturday morning to a most hostile reception. Our instructions were to use the Sergeants Mess with sleeping quarters in the Officers Mess. At midday we wandered over to the Sergeants Mess for lunch, only to be turned away at the door by two old sweats. They were in a fearful temper and in no uncertain terms told us that as LAC we were not permitted to enter their 'Holy of Holies'.

We were the first wartime intake to arrive at Shawbury. All previous pupils had been officers or sergeant pilots from the RAFVR. Even when the Adjutant arrived, (who was, incidentally, Henry Cotton the golfer) the sergeants still held out and we were forced to eat in the Airmens Mess. In the station orders on the Monday, the CO stated that all training aircrew were promoted to acting sergeant. This infuriated the old diehards who resorted to such petty techniques as hiding the newspapers and taking up several seats when we went into the ante-room.

In Thursday's station orders all sergeant pilots were told to use an ante-room in the Officers Mess. So we ended up living in the Officers Mess and eating in the Sergeants Mess, running a gauntlet of dirty looks every time we appeared for a meal. It took many months for some of the old station sergeants to accept that there was a war on and things had to be different from peacetime. Being made acting sergeants was beneficial for more than just overcoming opposition within our own side however. Should we be taken prisoner of war it ensured that we would be sent to camps for non-commissioned officers and could expect better treatment than in a camp for lower ranks.

My instructor at Shawbury was the Flight OC, Flt Lt Nicoll. He was very typical of pre-war RAF, a chap who enjoyed life to the full and he would often come over to our watering hole in Shrewsbury. He would be completely relaxed in our company but we always respected his rank. Later on I was surprised to find that the Canadians and Australians often totally disregarded rank and in social circumstances would immediately start calling an officer by his christian name.

We were now flying Oxfords which I found to be quite temperamental with their slight swing on take-off although they were good preparation for my later encounters with the Beaufighter and its vicious swing. The pattern of flying at Shawbury was chaotic. The intake of pupils had been doubled from ten to twenty in each of the four flights and the numbers of aircraft were a constant hazard to each other. We would taxi to the take-off side and have to quickly judge where our best chances of a clear take-off path lay. Having positioned ourselves we would wait for a slot with engines heating all the while, anxious to become airborne before any approaching aircraft hit us from behind. I remember that quite often on the point of take-off I would spot another Oxford aborting his attempt because my aircraft had taken his path.

In much the same way on landing it was a case of picking a clear piece of airfield and just hoping that nobody else was coming in on it at the same time. After landing we would make straight for the perimeter hedge and only then was it safe to turn and taxi back to the hangers, closely hugging the hedgeside. There were no hard and fast rules about who had right of way in these manoeuvres and never a day went by without a collision on the ground, leading to many friendly arguments over who was in the wrong.

I particularly enjoyed the instrument and night flying we did at Shawbury. As a child I had hated the dark and night flying presented me with a challenge to overcome this latent childhood fear. Stuck in the pitch black of the cockpit, surrounded by instruments it was up to me to get myself down on the ground in one piece. With a night landing I always felt a sense of self-achievement.

During my first couple of hours of dual night instruction, Flt Lt Nicoll and I came very close to disaster. An air raid warning early in the evening meant that all night instruction was delayed and, typical of Shawbury, commenced with a rush when it began. Our aircraft had not been filled with fuel and we had to sit in the cockpit while two fitters hastily removed the wing panel to get to the filler. They completed the job at great speed and once the bowser was clear, gave us the O.K. to start up.

I taxied to the flare path and having been given the all clear, prepared for take-off. Three quarters of the way down the flare path, past the point of no return, I realised that there was no way we were going to become airborne. My moment of panic passed as Flt Lt Nicoll calmly told me that he had taken control and he then proceeded to bounce the aircraft off the ground, telling me to lift the undercarriage as he did so. There was a hedge at the end of the flare path followed by a field and a big wood with high oaks and elms. As the first line of trees became visible in the moonlight our altimeter read just 80 feet. I am certain we brushed against branches as we passed over the edge of the wood. For about a minute we travelled with the speed stuck at 110 m.p.h. unable to gain height. My instructor's voice suddenly broke in on my confusion, calmly lecturing me on what to do in this situation. He told me that we must gain 200 feet before attempting a turn. After what seemed like hours but was just a matter of minutes the altimeter showed 200 feet and he turned the aircraft 90 degrees and positioned it for returning to the circuit. As we approached the downside of the circuit I was told to keep flashing the emergency code for permission to land. On giving us the all clear, the landing party stupidly put on the chance light when we were on the downside and left it on. We were still at only 200 feet and approaching the flare path with no undercarriage or flaps down. Flt Lt Nicoll ordered me to lower these during the very last seconds of descent and he made a perfect landing.

I was filled with relief and an overwhelming desire to shout my congratulations to Ft Lt Nicoll, but highly impressed by his unruffled demeanour throughout the episode, I decided to act nonchalantly too and say nothing. On arriving back at the flight hangar, the maintenance sergeant handed us our wing panel which had been removed for refuelling and not replaced. The two fitters were immediately put on a charge and the next day I was called to give evidence. Their negligence had endangered my life but I was pleased that they only received a reprimand because I felt partly to blame. I knew that a pilot should always check both the cockpit and the exterior of his aircraft before take-off and in the rush I had not done so.

As our 12-week course neared its end, I was once again facing the dreaded exams. The wing's written exam looked like being my major downfall. A scotsman, Sergeant Robson (Robbie) and I were both keen to fly twin-engine fighters and we teamed up as pilot and co-pilot. He was a third-year law student at Edinburgh University and somehow managed to help me through practical navigation and bomb targeting. He was a great friend and we went on to serve at the same Operational Training Unit where most distressingly, he and his crew were killed in an accident.

As it happened the RAF were just as keen that we passed the written exams as we were. The desks in the exam room were very close together and there was no limit on how many people disappeared off to the toilet at one time. It had also been made public knowledge well beforehand that smoking would be allowed during the exams. This meant the cigarette packets became handy little libraries. As a non-smoker I collected several empty packets of Players Twenty and having placed a single cigarette in each, crammed the remaining space with handwritten study aids. Throughout the exams I would scrabble in my pockets for the right packet with the relevant subject material hidden inside. Later on when the Empire Training Scheme was launched, the RAF became a great deal stricter concerning exam passes but luckily for me, with the early intakes they felt they needed everyone who showed a practical ability to fly.

Seventeen of the twenty pupils who had arrived at Shawbury received their wings. Only one person failed, the other two being

25

killed in an air collision. My results were above average for night flying, average for flying and a pass in the written exams. I did not receive one of the eight commissions granted which mostly went to the university graduates, but was pleased to be told by my Flight OC that I had been number nine. Apparently my written work was just not good enough – something I could hardly argue with!

I really wasn't too concerned about the lack of commission feeling that I would be happier arriving at a squadron along with a lot of sprog sergeants and have to prove my worth. I felt that to arrive from flight training as an officer could lead to being regarded as a PO Prune. In fact I found this was often the case, that when newly commissioned officers arrived fresh from training school they were deemed as slightly inferior and found it hard to have orders obeyed. However, I was happy for those of my colleagues who did make the grade and celebrated on their behalf. I had made some true friends during my training and could never have imagined how many would loose their lives in the course of the war. One friend in particular deserves a mention, Ian MacRobert. I count myself lucky to have met Ian with whom I shared many raucous nights. He never let on that his eldest brother had been killed in a flying accident and tragically a few months after training, both Ian and his remaining brother were reported missing. His mother donated three Spitfires to the war effort in memory of her sons and later a Sterling bomber named 'The MacRobert Reply'.

After we'd gained our wings, we were given the choice of heavy bombers, medium bombers or twin-engine fighters. We knew that there was a big call for medium bombers as losses had been high since Dunkirk but I was still set on twin-engine fighters and put them as first choice ahead of medium bombers and finally heavy bombers. I was delighted to be allocated my first choice and joined Robbo, whose decision had been identical to me, on the journey to Catfoss in Yorkshire where we had been posted to the Operational Training Unit. Catfoss had both long and short-nosed fighter Blenheims.

6

On arrival we were told that due to bad weather there was a log-jam of training and the eight of us due to start on twin-engine fighters were being posted to Squiresgate at Blackpool. We were to fly Ansons loaded with trainee navigators, around the Irish Sea. Our fury at this change was further compounded when we could receive no answer as to how long we would spend at Squiresgate. We caught a train to Blackpool and found that we were billeted in a boarding house on the front. Our landlady greeted our arrival with a lecture on house rules before showing us to our room. All eight of us were to sleep in one room, four in the double bed and four in camp beds. We threw our kit bags onto the tiny floor space available and headed out to drown our sorrows. Things began to look up when we realised that the boarding house was only a stone's throw from the Tower Ballroom and that Blackpool was alive and buzzing. A number of companies had evacuated the South for Blackpool and the town was also the receiving centre for RAF ground staff. There was quite a stir when we entered the Winter Gardens that first night, the only sergeant pilots among hundreds of AC 2s.

Our sojourn in Blackpool lasted for a glorious fortnight during which time even I managed to drag myself away from the bar and onto the dance floor on two or three occasions. In fact one night I was even foolish enough to pay for a taxi to take myself and a popsie home. At the end of the week we were all broke but managed to keep going by borrowing. We had at first agreed to make a point of all arriving back at the boarding house at the same time each night to facilitate getting to bed. This rule was quickly forgotten and there was little sleep for anyone as the early hours were punctuated with different bods arriving and trying to find their sleeping place.

Flying Ansons when tired and hungover was no pleasure. The Anson was a ropy aircraft. To lift the undercarriage we had to turn a handle 147 times. A foot pump was then used to build the air pressure for the brakes but by the time the aircraft had taxied around the perimeter of the airfield for take-off, the air had often run out and back we would go for further pumping. The vibration was tremendous causing the windows to rattle. Once airborne the handling was not too bad but in our severely weakened state, the horrors of take-off were torturous. Thank goodness we were recalled to Catfoss after the second week. We were all seriously broke and in desperate need of sleep.

Back in the cockpit of a two-engine aircraft, a short-nosed Blenheim, I experienced a few moments of panic. The double bank of instruments suddenly appeared totally confusing, how would I cope on my own? I wasn't given much time to worry though, after only a couple of hours we were sent up solo in Mark IVs. The armament was the same for both Mark Is and Mark IVs, six Brownings at the front with one Lewis gun in the turret.

Soon after going solo I managed to get myself placed on my first charge, thanks to a brainless building contractor. I had been practising take-off and landing in the morning and after lunch went out to resume my practice. A load of bricks had mysteriously appeared at the end of the runway but I didn't take much notice of them, confident that nobody would tip bricks in the obvious path of aircraft. I carried out my cockpit drill, taxied down the runway, turned 180 degrees and heard the most amazing crunch. Surprisingly the damage was slight, a six-inch rip in the rudder and within five minutes the sergeant rigger had fixed the hole with some fabric and dope. Unfortunately the Chief Flying Instructor spotted the aircraft grounded and came over to see what the problem was. He completely lost his temper and placed me on a charge. The next day I went up before him and was treated to ten minutes of verbal abuse and confined to camp for three days. The fact that the bricks should never have been there and that the damage was minimal, costing less than one pound to repair made no difference. Furious, I determined to hunt down the contractor and tell him what to do with his bricks, but luckily for him he had quickly finished his work and departed.

Two weeks after we'd commenced training at Catfoss our eight observers arrived. We were officially introduced to them in the crew room although we'd actually chanced upon them the night before in the mess and had already teamed up over a few beers. My observer was to be Des Owen. Robbo and I were already in a room meant to hold two crews so now there were four of us, waiting for the airgunners to turn up.

The day they did arrive was a disastrous one for me. We were using Driffield Aerodome, or what was left of it after a severe bomb attack in September, as a satellite. I was over there putting in some practice in a Blenheim when I made the grave mistake of lowering the flaps instead of the undercarriage when coming in to land. In my defence I would like to point out that in the Blenheim the two levers for lowering undercarriage and flaps were positioned to the right of the pilot and only eight inches apart. We were taught never to look for a lever but to do it all by feel and the positioning made this rather difficult. However it was still my error and within a couple of seconds I realised what I had done and raised the flaps and lowered the undercarriage. I just thought I had made a small mistake and that was the end of that. As I reached the final approach and the correct time to lower the flaps, the aircraft swung violently to port and tried to roll over. I managed to correct this but had to land with full right rudder and full aileron to prevent a roll. The aircraft was moving like a crab and swung to port again on touchdown but I struggled to straighten out by using the engines. I parked by the watch office and reported the problem to the sergeant rigger, not even thinking to mention my error with the flaps, before disappearing into the crew room. After only a few minutes, the sergeant rigger came and took me back to the aircraft. Underneath the starboard wing the flaps were swinging loosely with all their hydraulic stays broken. I suddenly realised what had happened and began a garbled account to the rigger but he silenced me by telling me he knew exactly what had happened and that usually the result was a fatal spin. I felt incredibly foolish and much appreciated his suggestion that he wouldn't report the incident but would just get a new set of stays from stores and have the aircraft ready for service that evening.

So I was perhaps not in the best of moods when I walked into the mess at Catfoss that evening and was met by an unfamiliar airgunner who told me he was on my crew. His appearance completely took me back. He looked as if he hadn't had a wash for a week, his hair was dishevelled and his uniform unclean. Apparently the eight wireless operator gunners had arrived that morning and the other seven pilots had quickly crewed up, leaving me with this obvious mismatch. Des Owen agreed that there was something rather odd about him, a feeling that was confirmed that evening when he invited himself along for a drink with us. He spent the entire evening chasing every female in the pub, in between spinning us long yarns about his great ability as a wireless operator gunner.

The next morning I felt I had no choice but to go to the Flight Commander and say that this chap wouldn't fit in with our crew. The Flight Commander commiserated with me but said there were no spare gunners and I would have to give him a chance. During training his ability to use the wireless, both transmitting and receiving, was deplorable and his gunnery was just as bad. When we tested him out I must admit that I threw the Blenheim about unmercifully over the target area but it was quite obvious that he couldn't hit a haystack. The Flight Commander was well aware of our problems but explained that while at Operational Training Unit it was impossible to obtain another crew member and it would be best to wait until we got to a squadron. In the meantime we put up with him as best we could.

Luckily this gunner was not with us when a group of us managed to have five days unofficial leave in Hull. It was on a snowy Saturday night in December and we had been to a party in the town and missed the last bus back to Catfoss. We made our way to a taxi rank only to be told that the snow was drifting too badly for a car to go that far. The Salvation Army hostel took us in for the night and the next morning we rang the camp. The camp was completely cut off and the Adjutant advised us to stay in Hull, saying that the RAF would reimburse all our living expenses. On the Sunday evening we booked into a hotel but even by pooling our money we realised we couldn't stay for more than one night. So it was back to the Salvation Army. We were marooned in Hull until the Friday and became well known by the publicans who were most generous to our plight. The RAF never did reimburse our expenses, blaming us for not leaving Hull at the first sign of snow, but we made sure the pubs were all paid back. In spite of the inclement weather and the lack of funds our visit to Hull had made a pleasant break.

It was soon after this incident that Robbo and his crew were killed. The crash was something of a mystery but occurred when he was doing an advanced square search in the North Sea. Just before he was due to take-off he came running into the crew room and asked if he could borrow my wrist watch as his was on the blink. I never hesitated in handing it over to him although it was something of a prized possession, being a Rolex Oyster which my godfather had given me for my 21st birthday only a few months previously. A crowd of us were going to a pub in Hornsea that evening and as he left the room Robbo shouted that he and his crew wouldn't make the six o'clock bus but would be on the later one.

Nobody was unduly worried when none of Robbo's crew had arrived a few hours later, even when it was realised that they were two hours overdue at camp. On arriving back and seeing the three empty beds I guessed they must have force landed somewhere and would be back as soon as they could. It was a complete shock when the next morning we were told the aircraft had been found in hills in the Peak District. To get to their destination in the North Sea they would have flown to Beverley, then due south to Gainsborough, then due east to pass through a corridor just north of Maplethorpe and out into the North Sea. Quite literally, to end up in the Peak District, they must have taken a right instead of a left at Gainsborough, but how this could have happened with two excellent men in the pilot and navigator on board I do not know. Even the airgunner had done some pilot training.

This was my first experience of losing a close friend to the war and I felt quite devastated by the suddenness of it all. We were all well aware of the dangers of flying but it brought home with great force how easily we could be here today and gone tomorrow. For the rest of the course I had to sleep in a room with three empty beds so that every night and every morning I was reminded of the sad fate of three wonderful friends.

A few days after the accident I went to see the Adjutant about the whereabouts of my watch. Although it sounds terribly mercenary, a good watch was quite hard to come by and in a way its return would have been a memento of Robbo. The Adjutant, who's responsibility it was to return all personal effects to the next of kin, said that a watch had been found and sent on to Robbo's father. He was sympathetic but unable to comment further and suggested that I write to Mr Robson if I wished to lay claim to it. This sounded far too mercenary. I did not know Mr Robson and if he questioned my claim I felt my friendship with his late son would be blighted. I decided to forget about it and it was certainly only a minor hiccup compared with what was to come in later years.

7

We did not actually complete our course, being short of one night flight which we were unable to fit in due to air raids. Nonetheless we were deemed fit for operations and posted to our squadrons. I was one of two crews sent to 248 Squadron at Dyce near Aberdeen. The pilot of the other crew was a rather strange chap, who I always suspected was not keen on his job. He came from Liverpool and was forever requesting compassionate leave on receiving letters from various family members who all seemed to suffer dreadfully in the bombing raids. Soon after arriving at Dyce he disappeared from the station.

Six months later, I was on detachment to Carew Cheriton in South Wales and walked into the watch office to come face to face with the same chap, acting as a permanent duty pilot. There were one or two pilots who having obtained their wings went looking for cushy jobs like this. Having got your wings, nobody could take them from you, something I totally disagreed with in such a case. Needless to say, he didn't know where to put himself when he saw me but I just filled out my required movements and left. Actually he did me a favour by his behaviour. His airgunner, Johnny Rushforth, was decidedly fed up and asked me if he could join my crew. I was only too delighted to ditch my airgunner, so with a few words in the right places, Johnny joined my crew and proved to be excellent at his job.

I think just about everybody felt like a new boy at school on joining a squadron but it didn't take long to settle. Our squadron was without a CO and was being run by the Flight Commanders.

We were in A Flight with Flt. Lt. MacHardy DFC as OC. He was a New Zealander who came to Britain a few years before war broke out and took a short service commission. Being the first of the wartime volunteers to join the squadron, I felt at first that we were lacking in hours. The RAF tended to judge your ability on the number of hours you had flown although this was rather misleading. I remember one chap at ITW who boasted of having flown several hundred hours in the course of the Spanish Civil War, only to fail trying to fly Oxfords.

The squadron was more or less resting when we arrived, having had a rough time when down at Bircham Newton during the autumn, bombing shipping off the Dutch and German coast. They had scrapped the bomb racks and just had fighter Blenheims with the six Browning and the turret Lewis guns. Most of the work was providing escorts for the Atlantic convoys as they came in range of the Northern Approaches.

We were soon moved up to Wick, the only squadron of Blenheims among the Hudson and Whitley squadrons which were busy carrying out anti-submarine patrols. At this time the convoys were coming under attack from the long range Focke Wulf Condor and it was our job to give the convoy cover during its last 300 miles. I found this terribly monotonous even though I understood the importance. We were usually airborne for about seven hours and I actually never encountered a Condor which was perhaps just as well for the Condors were much faster than the Blenheims and unless spotted early could move in, bomb and go before the Blenheim could reach him. I don't think any Condors were shot down by Blenheims but I suppose our presence gave the Merchant Navy moral support.

The Mercury engines did not seem to like the Scottish weather. I remember one morning I was due to take off about two hours before daylight so as to arrive over the convoy at first light. It was incredibly cold with sleet lashing down on the wings and I had to try three aircraft before I hit upon a serviceable engine. Such delays were enough to rattle anybody's nerves. Racing against time we would climb into one aircraft and I would go through the cockpit drill while the observer unpacked his bag and set out his maps, only to find the engines would not start and we must pack up and run to another aircraft.

I defy any pilot to say that he didn't get butterflies before a take-off on operations, regardless of whether everything went smoothly or not. Following the briefing I would leave the operations room and I had an understanding with my observers that I would be in the met room leaving them to plot the courses. I always found I felt a lot calmer away from the ops room. Talk was usually fairly strained as we made our way out to the aircraft and it was not until we were taxiing for take-off that the stomach gremlins would disappear. Even when we were full speed down the runway, when several things could have gone wrong, I would be relaxed. It was the whole procedure of getting started that was so nerve-racking.

There were only a couple of occasions when I failed to find the convoy and this was always due to poor weather conditions. I remember one day I had orders to pick up a naval force well north of Cape Wrath. As we were flying due north I could see a vigorous front ahead, very dark and menacing. We entered it at 1,000 feet and quickly hit heavy snow. Ice began to build up on the wings and I could see that we were not going to be able to pass through. As I carried out a 180 degree turn I realised that the air speed was dropping and the aircraft had become very sluggish. It seemed an age before we finally came out into the clear. The noise of the lumps of ice falling off the wings and hitting the fuselage and tail was deafening. In an attempt to reach our destination I climbed to 17,000 feet and tried to fly over the top of the front, but it reached far above us and we were forced to abort the operation.

The Hudsons were not a popular aircraft. At Wick we were billeted in married quarters close to the east/west runway and there were a number of times when I was woken by the howling noise of the Pratt and Whitney engines as they tried to get off the ground. This was followed by the whoosh of an explosion as the aircraft failed to make take-off. There only needed to be a slight bump for the undercart to collapse, which could easily pierce the wings. The wings contained all the fuel in unstrengthened tanks and so there was a huge risk of explosion. A bad landing could also trigger off fatal results. Sometimes the crews did get out in time but more often they hadn't a hope. We used to be amazed at all the press photos used as propaganda, showing merchant ships arriving from

America with the decks packed with Hudsons wing-tip to wing-tip. When all was said and done, they were built as a passenger craft for medium hauls, not to be loaded with bombs and a turret.

Whitleys were another fairly unpopular aircraft and it was while I was at Wick that I saw a horrifying crash involving a Whitley. We had finished our day's flying and coming out of the debriefing looked up to see a Whitley lumbering over us with all its navigational lights on. It was obviously in trouble and as we watched the pilot flew a large circuit and made a long approach for landing, taking him over Wick town. He was rapidly loosing height and as he came over the edge of the town there was an enormous explosion and an instant fireball. We realised with horror that he must have hit the hospital. By the time we got to the scene one wing of the hospital, the nurses quarters, was fully ablaze. Luckily the quarters had been fairly empty at the time but tragically there were five deaths in addition to the loss of the Whitley crew.

The endorsement I acquired at Wick was gained while flying a Blenheim and was totally my own fault. We were returning from a trip late in the evening and the flare path would not give me a signal to land. I circled round and round until I was almost dizzy and the fuel was running low. I was very aware that we were all due to go on leave the next morning and that we had to get our travel vouchers and leave passes that evening in order to catch the only train from Wick to Aberdeen which went at 0600 hours. As the time neared 2200 hours I decided that I should try to land without the flare path, reasoning that there must be an air raid alert. It was a beautiful moonlit night and I could just see the outline of the runway. At the very last minute of descent I flicked the landing light on and just as I was feeling rather pleased with myself, I saw the wreckage of a crashed Hudson strewn across the runway. My only option was to ground loop the Blenheim and in so doing we ran off the runway and the undercart collapsed.

I made my way to the ops room for debriefing with a very heavy heart. Sure enough I was placed on open arrest. The Station Commander had apparently seen what had happened and was furious. Our leave was automatically cancelled and another crew took our place. The leave roster was so tightly scheduled that a hitch like this meant we had to go the bottom and would have to wait another 12 weeks. I argued that it was unfair on my observer and airgunner, after all it had been my decision to land, but it was to no avail and the three of us had to remain in camp. I must say both Johnny Rushford and Des Owen took it extremely well, although they didn't fail to point out that I would now owe them several beers.

The next day I duly appeared before the station CO who had luckily had time to cool down. In fact he gave me a rather fatherly lecture on the cost of repairing the aircraft and the fact that it would be out of service for a week. He concluded that he had no alternative but to give me an endorsement and warned me that next time I felt like breaking the rules I should remember that it cost my crew their leave, something I was not likely to forget in a hurry.

A few weeks after this incident, I had another lucky escape in a Blenheim when one of my engines failed. We were doing a continuous day patrol along the coast of Norway, from Skagerrak to Bergen and as there was forecast 8/10 cloud at 1,000 feet, we carried it out using the cloud cover. We were just finishing our patrol when we lost power in the port engine. We limped home with one full engine and one giving about 20 per cent power. It seemed an awful long way to Wick that night.

The social life was somewhat limited at Wick as it was a teetotal town with the nearest pub 25 miles down the road. The only drink we could get was from an old distillery and this involved real cloak and dagger drama. The manager of the distillery, who ran it as a watering hole to line his own pocket, asked us to enter the yard alone, or at the most in pairs, to avoid raising suspicions. It was not the police he feared but local residents. He kept a good stock of Youngers beers and had a ready trade with the aerodrome. I never saw a local there and could not say where they nipped off to for a crafty drink. I can only remember one dance and social evening in the Sergeants' mess with girls outnumbered by men by four to one. There were very few WAAF on the station and Wick itself was bereft of females who all seemed to have moved south.

8

I must admit I was pleased when at last our squadron also moved south. We went to Bircham Newton in Norfolk. I knew this part of Norfolk well from peacetime and was only 15 minutes flying time from the farm. Our move thankfully meant that our regular convoy escort was more or less finished. Instead we flew continuous patrols and reconnaissance along the German, Dutch and Danish coasts, either at sea level, or where possible using cloud cover. There was very little cover in those months of May and June 1941 however, which were gloriously sunny and hot.

The patrol I enjoyed most was the one at last light when ships would appear from port to slip along the coast during darkness. Having taken a reading of their position we would move clear of the coast and climb to about 1,500 feet. From that height we could radio a message back to base and the torpedo boats would then be alerted and make their dash across the North Sea.

Soon after our arrival we acquired a new squadron CO and a PO navigator. The CO had done one tour and was thought to be on a rest period for he never did an operation on Blenheims. The PO navigator turned out to be John Dearden, a chap I knew fairly well before the war and who had more recently just married a cousin of mine. As the squadron was short of a navigational officer he was immediately appointed, something which did not go down well with older members of the squadron, some of whom were near to finishing a tour. He further alienated himself by sharing a house with the new squadron CO and his wife in a village about three miles from camp. John had private means and could afford this luxury for himself and Angela.

I remained fairly unconcerned by the gossip surrounding John's arrival but looked forward to meeting him and Angela, as I had shared many childhood holidays with the latter. I was somewhat surprised therefore by his behaviour on our first meeting. He called me into his office about a week after his arrival and being only a sergeant, I saluted him and called him 'Sir' as a sign of respect to his commission. He told me to stand at ease and I then expected some sort of informal chat, or at least to be addressed by my christian name. Instead he asked me when the compass on the aircraft I usually flew had last been swung. I answered that this had been carried out the previous week and he then told me to get it done again within the next 48 hours. I saluted and gave him a smart 'Yes, sir', but I was still half expecting him to start laughing at the absurdity of our situation. After all, the last time we'd met, in January 1940, we'd both had a few to drink and had had a great evening.

Unfortunately, John's rise through the ranks seemed to have gone to his head somewhat and during his time at Bircham Newton he continued to act as if we had never set eyes on each other before. For my part I always respected his King's commission and would salute whenever we met, although I must admit my salutes were rather elaborate and exaggerated as I found the situation slightly farcical. I was quite hurt though by Angela's lack of attempt to contact me. It was only after they'd moved from Bircham Newton that I heard from her. After the Beaufighters were introduced John was posted to Beauforts at Thorney Island and shortly after, went missing. Angela contacted me to see if I could find out anything about his disappearance. She was convinced he had been taken prisoner of war. As it happened, a Beaufort from his squadron was diverted to Bircham Newton and I was able to talk to the crew. They told me that John's aircraft had been hit in a raid and on coming down had become entangled in cables and exploded. All this had happened in France. I broke this news as carefully as I could to Angela, but like so many other relatives who heard that a loved one had gone missing, she clung to the hope that he was a prisoner of war.

By now the Blenheims were definitely showing signs of being past their sell-by-date. It became almost common practice to have to pull the Plus Nine Boost to get them off the ground. This Plus Nine Boost was meant for emergency use only. It was a soft wire that was broken by the action of a lever and could only run for two and a half minutes. Once it was broken it had to be reported to the Engineering Officer and the engine was meant to be taken out and stripped down. As more serviceability from each aircraft was the order of the day, a blind eye was often turned to this requirement.

One afternoon three Beaufighters arrived and we were told that we would remain operational with the Blenheims but were to be converted to Beaus within a fortnight. The next few weeks were hectic. I vividly remember the first time I swung up into the pilot's seat, a feat which in itself demanded you were something of a gymnast. Two parallel bars were positioned above the pilot's seat and the pilot had to swing up onto them in order to lower himself into the seat. Cockpit drill seemed terrifying as I gazed at the double bank of instruments, levers and switches and wondered how on earth I would memorise what each one did. After about three hours, I felt slightly more confident about it all and had familiarised myself with the layout of the aircraft – now to actually fly it. As it was impossible to have dual controls, it was a case of standing in the well behind an officer, who in my case had only gone solo himself the previous day, and watch what he did as he flew a circuit and landed. It was then up to me to get in and fly.

The Beaufighter really was a dream of an aircraft. I'll never forget on that first solo flight, the tremendous kick as I opened up and got the full thrust of 3,000 horsepower. I was over the next parish by the time I'd checked everything on take-off. The servo controls meant that landing was perfectly straightforward and really there were only two negative points about the aircraft. One of these was its habit to swing on take-off and again if landing on a short distance and the other was the procedure to bale out. According to the manufacturer's manual, the pilot had to pull the catch on the hatch door, lower his backrest and roll head over heels backwards into the well. From here he had to struggle through the hatch, complete with parachute. The windscreen emergency panel to the left of the pilot was not recommended for baling out as he would fall straight in front of the tailplane which would decapitate him on impact. The observer stood a slightly better chance of survival as he only had to get through the floor hatch, but I never did hear of either a pilot or an observer safely baling out from a Beau. Very soon we were receiving brand new Beaufighters which were coming straight from the manufacturers, given a day's squadron check and passed directly on to us.

The only true drawback to the arrival of the Beaus was that all our observers and airgunners were posted to heavy and medium bombers. I thoroughly enjoyed the farewell parties we held in The Globe in King's Lynn but was sad to say goodbye to Des Owen and Johnny Rushford. They were both posted to Beauforts but tragically neither saw the end of their tour.

The old Blenheims were being sent down to Cunliffe Owen at Southampton Airport where they were refurbished and sent on to the Middle East. One day five fellow pilots were detailed to deliver Blenheims down to Southampton and I was to take a further aircraft to bring them all back in. We were to stay overnight at the Polygon Hotel; what a bash it would be. Unfortunately among the five was a flight sergeant, Reg Jones, who came from Southampton and whom I disliked intensely. He had treated me very much as a new boy when I first arrived with the squadron and was constantly bragging about the number of ops he had flown. He was also a teetotaller, something which did not endear him to many of the lads and had only one ambition, to gain a commission.

When I arrived down in Southampton I was horrified to find that he had organised for us all to have dinner with his parents. The others had agreed, thinking we could go out later, but I was most dubious about the whole thing. It was just as awful as I had expected. His father was a chapel preacher who was also teetotal and after a meal washed down with cocoa he suggested a game of whist. If we had to play a game we'd rather it had been poker but what we wanted was to leave and it was quite obvious that they thought we were staying the night. Unable to stand it any longer, I suggested that we were due to go out for a drink. Undaunted Mr Jones produced three bottles of beer to be shared between us. To crown it all we ended up dossing down in armchairs and on the floor for the night – a far cry from our five-star hotel.

The next morning, over tea and toast, Reg informed his parents that as he was the most senior in terms of flying hours, he would be flying us all back to Norfolk. This was the final straw for me and I quickly retorted that I had been detailed by the Flight Commander to fly the Blenheim and that was what I would be doing. The others all backed me on this, but right up until we reached the airfield he ranted on about how he should be flying. I ignored him and went to the watch officer for clearance. I did however add insult to injury by allowing him to be navigator, a just reward I felt for having put us through such a miserable evening and for his behaviour to me when I first joined the squadron. Aside from this petty squabble, I did feel a heavy sense of responsibility in flying six operational pilots, all packed into any available space including the turret, fuselage and tail. The runway was far from long, being a pre-war civil airfield, and threequarters of the way along it I realised that the Blenheim was not going to make it. I quickly pulled the Plus Nine Boost lever towards me and felt the aircraft shudder as it hauled itself into the air. I am quite certain that over the noise of the engines, I heard five people sigh with relief!

Soon after the departure of our old crews, 20 observer wireless operators arrived on the squadron. This was a new trade specially created for Beaufighters. The observers had volunteered to take a wireless course and their brevet was the half wing with the letters OP. Each pilot was allocated an OP with the hope that you would stick together as a team. Having suffered the traumas of such a mismatched airgunner as I initially had at Catfoss, I approached this new navigator with some trepidation. I needn't have worried. Richard Hutchinson was a broad Scot from Dundee with a terrific sense of humour. In civvy street he was a chartered surveyor, and unmarried I was pleased to hear. His first question to me was to ask what sort of pilot I was. When I replied that I was a pretty ropy one he said that was just the sort he was looking for. I was to become very used to his good-natured sarcasm which he never failed to employ when I made even the slightest of mistakes. On the occasions when our landing was less than perfect, I could guarantee there'd be a short silence followed by the muttered phrase, 'What a bloody arrival.'

42

Hutch was also an excellent navigator who regarded with scorn the use of the wireless for directions. Many a time I would ask him for a bearing or fix and he would snap back that if I wasn't satisfied with his dead reckoning then he would go and crew up with another pilot. He never did and we stayed together throughout.

The reason I was pleased he was unmarried was simply because I found that the fewer attachments anybody had, the more committed they were to their work. As a two-man crew it also helped if we remained close friends on the ground as well as when we were flying and this was not usually possible with a married man. I always found that those who lacked the strong moral fibre needed at this time were generally married, especially those who married while on leave. It stood to reason that your flying could be affected if you were worried about your own safety because of the effect on your wife. In the same vein it did not seem fair on a wife to have such a strain put on her. In fact my only concern with Hutch was that he could not swim. This was not unusual in those days as it was not something taught in schools and public pools were not common. I was always very aware of the dangers if we had to ditch over the sea and we therefore devised our own ditching drill in which Hutch had a chance to jump straight into the dinghy without so much as wetting his feet. This was to come in very useful in a few months' time.

During conversion we sadly lost one crew to a foolish bet. Over lunch one day in the Officers Mess a light-hearted discussion on how to roll a Beau developed into a challenge as to who would be the first to do so. That afternoon, PO Birtles took an aircraft up for an air test with a ground crew member and having only completed two or three hours in Beaufighters, stupidly attempted to roll the aircraft. The tailplane was ripped off and both men were killed. The Beau was capable of rolling but only in very experienced hands. I remember seeing Wing Commander Staniforth roll at 500 feet over Portreath aerodrome on his way to the Middle East. Several pilots still tried to carry out this manoeuvre though. I was once asked by a pilot with less experience than myself to test his aircraft as he suspected that a certain pilot had tried to roll it. It was a horrible flight with the aircraft moving like a crab and needing trimming every five minutes. It had obviously been strained.

The only other prang during conversion involved the squadron CO himself. During a practice flight both engines cut and he was forced to crash-land in a field with the wheels up. This was due to pilot error as on inspection it was found that the outer tanks of both engines were dry and the cocks had not been turned over to the inner tanks. An enquiry was to be held but the CO covered for himself well. As my Southampton friend had been the last one to fly the aircraft the CO got him to say that he told the fitter that only the outer tanks required filling and that the fitter had signed the 700 and then forgotten to fill the tanks. The CO was cleared of all blame at the enquiry, the fitter was severely reprimanded and lo and behold within a month my Southampton pal got a commission.

9

When the full consignment of Beaus was completed each pilot was given an aircraft. I was allocated A for Angela, each aircraft being given a girl's name for radio identification. She was perfect, very docile with very little swing and a dream to fly; I hardly ever had to trim her in flight. I think we all formed quite an attachment to our own aircraft, partly I suppose because we realised that our lives depended on their reliability. I quite believed A for Angela had her own perfume of dope, oil and high octane hidden in her fuselage and I was immensely proud that she never failed to start and I never had to change aircraft after running up and carrying out a cockpit check before going on ops. Amongst the aircraft of that generation I still think the Beau had a proud, bulldog look with its high nose and tough looking lines.

Both A for Angela and I were very lucky to have a dedicated ground crew. One morning I arrived at the field to find that all the rows of exposed rivets along the aircraft had been covered with fabric, stuck on with dope. When my ground crew saw me examining his handy work he came over to say that I should get an extra ten miles per hour from this streamlining. He had spent all his free time the previous evening doing this cover up. Unfortunately after some steep turns and dives while practising attacks with another Beau, A for Angela looked as if she had been to a dance and had been festooned with paper streamers. The strips of fabric had all come loose with the airflow and were trailing all over the aircraft. My ground crew had one more go but eventually agreed that the rivets would have to remain exposed.

As Bircham Newton was only ten minutes flying time from the farm I would often fly home while doing conversion flying or an air test. I would go low over the fields to see how the crops were doing and then beat up the house, being careful that there were no horses working close by. I had no need of stamps for my letters home as I would just pop a note in a tobacco tin, attach a strip of fabric and drop it over the farm. For these 'bombing runs', Hutch would stand over the flare chute and when I shouted, he would throw the tin down the chute. Some of these runs were most successful although other letters were somewhat old news by the time they were read, only being discovered when the crops were cut at harvest.

One day I could not spot my father on the farm and thought he may be at an Observer Corps post set up on my uncle's farm, just outside the village. On one side of the field containing the post there was a long line of elm trees. I went out about two miles dropping to roof level and creeping up behind the post. I rose straight in front of those on duty which must have given them an awful shock and then went into a climbing turn so that my aircraft number could not be seen. It turned out that my father was not on duty and the two who were, hastily reported a low flying Beaufighter. Luckily they were friends of the family and after a few minutes suddenly realised that it had probably been me. They did me a very good turn by being just as quick to report that they had been mistaken and seen nothing. Their control room must have thought they were having a quiet tipple, stuck out there in the fens!

The squadron was now more or less operational with Beaufighters and ready for our first job. Four of us were ordered to Detling in Kent for a few days to test the Beau against small shipping that was occasionally slipping through the Straits of Dover in daylight. The day after our arrival, three of us were called to the ops room and briefed that there were five ships moving just off the French coast. FO Morris was to lead with myself as number two and another Sgt pilot as number three. To our surprise we were given an escort of two squadrons of Spitfires which arrived just as we were taking off. We hedge-hopped to the coast and dropped down over the cliffs of Dover to sea level to cross the Channel. On hitting the French coastline there was no sign of our target so we turned south, flying along the shoreline until we reached Calais harbour where we sighted the five ships. The Spits remained outside the harbour, ready to escort us home. We could see that these were flak ships, heavily-armoured for the protection of the Merchant Navy and it was a case of picking our own target. I chose the second ship on the left and giving the aircraft very nearly full throttle took it up to 100 feet where I could get a better bead on the bridge of the ship. By this time we were being fired at not only from the ships but also from shore guns, and I must say that I felt a hell of a lot better when my guns were firing in return.

I lifted the aircraft over the masts only to meet a renewed onslaught from the shore batteries. I knew that on no account must I turn away and expose the belly of the aircraft so I kept at rooftop level over Calais. Luckily there were no balloons as we raced across the town and all the tracer was coming from behind which meant they were unable to get a bead on us having been taken by surprise. Once we were out of the firing range Hutch's voice came over the intercom telling me to set a course north and then west to get out to sea again. As always he had anticipated what I was doing and had come up with the right answer. This time the shore guns were totally surprised as they must have been looking westward out to sea and we only experienced one or two haphazard tracers in gaining the Channel. Hutch was soon telling me a course for home and I took it, not expecting to see the Spits again as we were a good ten miles north of where we had left them.

Once landed we had to go straight to the debriefing room. On the walk over there neither Hutch nor myself said very much. It had been a fairly hairy first operation with the Beaus and I know that I was feeling a definite sense of relief. This was accentuated when Hutch told me that he had seen number three turn after the attack, which made him an easy target to be hit, and he had crashed. The debriefing by the intelligence officer was very thorough as this was the first op with the Beau against shipping. I am sure that he wanted to hear that we had left at least one ship sinking, but all we could claim was an extensive amount of bridge damage. A few days later we heard through French intelligence that the ships had had to be withdrawn for repairs, so our first operation had been fairly successful.

Our fortnight at Detling coincided with the first anniversary of the start of the Battle of Britain and the hospitality of the people was quite unbelievable. We were usually stood down by 1900 hours and would then make our way to a pub in Maidstone. Before we knew what was happening, rounds of beers would appear at our table.

On our return to Bircham Newton we found that seven crews had been posted to the Middle East, leaving plenty of spare aircraft as they collected new ones to fly out in. We had also acquired a new Flight Commander, Dave Cartridge. He was a regular and it was his first tour as he had been instructing at FTS.

A few days later I was sent down to Carew Cheriton with Flt Lt Cartridge. We were told that we were to carry out a most important job, but no details were forthcoming. After a three-day wait we were briefed to escort a civil aircraft. We were to rendezvous over Lundy Isle at 0600 hours. We were not to formate on the aircraft and were to keep at least 75 yards from it. We were not given any courses that it would be flying, just told to go as far as we could with it. It was hinted that if an attack occurred and our guns jammed or for any other reason we could not shoot, then we were expected to ram the enemy aircraft. The civil aircraft was 90 minutes late over Lundy Isle. It then set a south-west course out into the Atlantic before turning south-east with its obvious destination being Gibraltar. Blinds were drawn down at every window and only the two pilots were visible. Having wasted 90 minutes fuel over Lundy Isle, we were not able to go as far as we had hoped.

Obviously we speculated over who was in the aircraft but it was not until a month later that news was released of Churchill's visit to troops in Egypt the previous month. All the facts pointed to us having accompanied his flight. Normally civilian flights to Gibraltar were carried out with very little hype and took a much straighter course. It was also unusual for escorts not to pick their aircraft up at the take-off point and the delays would indicate it was someone with a lot on his plate.

10

The day after we had escorted the civil aircraft, we were ordered down to Portreath in Cornwall where another crew from Bircham Newton joined us. We were attached to 10 Group, Fighter Command. Portreath was a jumping-off airfield for Gibraltar and the Middle East and hence a very busy aerodrome. There were also two squadrons of Polish Spitfires based there.

Flt Lt Cartridge was given the use of a Hillman van and all six of us used to pile into it for a night out. We all got on very well. Flt Lt Cartridge stood well over six feet tall and was a typical pre-war officer, even down to his pugnacious chin. He was the only officer amongst five Flt Sgts and Sgts and although he enjoyed our evenings out as much as anybody, woe betide the man who became overfamiliar and forgot his rank

On our first day at Portreath we were told to report to the control room where we met the Station Commanding Officer who outlined our duties. We were to be involved with a brand new project, the development of long-range interception (LRI). For some time the Air Ministry had been concerned about German aircraft having a free run into the Atlantic and North Sea from bases in France right up to Norway. Not only were these aircraft out of the range of our Spits and Hurricanes, they were also well clear of detection by Radio Telephone (R/T), which in those days was only about 80 to 90 miles. The enemy aircraft were therefore free to attack or shadow our convoys and ships.

British radar was fairly accurate at about 200 to 250 miles and the idea was that we would operate at these extremes. Instead of receiving the controller's directions verbally by R/T, as was the norm, our lifeline would be our Marconi receivers and transmitters. The navigators would receive a tapped-out message from the controller in the wireless cabin back at Portreath. He would then have to decipher the message and give the directions to the pilot. This was something we could really get out teeth into and we had the right officer in Flt Lt Cartridge, to lead us.

Two controllers were detailed to us and would work in close liaison with us, one would always be in command when we were flying. We found that a wireless cabin had been set up within shouting distance of the controller's interception table. If we were not on the interception we were expected to stand in the gallery and watch the controller at work, after which we were to give our opinions and suggestions. For the rest of the day the Station Signals Officer worked with the navigators showing them all the frequencies, wavebands etc, that they should be using. The navigators and their wirelesses were the key element for the success of the operation; as pilots we would be relying on their decoding of orders from the controller.

The ops room was just outside the camp and each time we went out there we had to pass Portreath Bay. Coming back on that first day, Flt Lt Cartridge suggested a swim in the strong Atlantic surf. It was really exhilarating, with not a soul about. We decided that we should go in everyday as a means of keeping fit and we did this right up until December. More often than not it was warmer in the sea than out of it. Poor Hutch joined us each day and tried hard to learn how to swim but the rough waves did not help him.

We had been allocated a corner of the airfield and our three Beaus were in bays close to the crew rooms and the CO's office. Three days after our arrival our ground staff joined us from Bircham Newton and we were able to fly. It took about a fortnight of training with the wireless. We would go about 200 miles off Land's End into the Bay of Biscay and fly at different heights to test for blind spots with the radar. There were a considerable number of these blind spots, not helped by the fact that our Marconi receiving and transmitting sets seemed to be housing a number of gremlins.

The controllers had devised a new code which was based on the fighter code but abbreviated by substituting the first letter of the word for the whole word. Thus Bandit became B and Angels 15,000 feet became A 150 etc. After our first disastrous attempted interception it was abundantly clear that too much time was being taken in passing the enemy position from the radar operators to the controller. He in turn was taking too long in deliberating the position. A five-second delay could mean a complete interception failure. It was a laborious process however with the radar position being given to the controller who then had to call out his interception to the wireless cabin who in turn had to code it and tap it out to our navigators.

Helped by practice and the enthusiasm of the radar people, controller, ops room staff and wireless cabin, which included the best looking WAAFs on the station, we managed to get our delay times down. It was a standard theory that it was not possible to see an enemy aircraft at a distance over two miles when at a height of 20,000 feet. Even then it was a help if there was cloud cover below to show him up.

When our fortnight's practice was over we were told that the next morning we were going to carry out the first long-range interception on an aircraft. The aircraft that had been chosen was one that appeared every morning on the radar screens at first light flying approximately 40 miles south-west of Brest out into the Atlantic. There were many theories as to where 'The Milk Train', as it was nicknamed, went. We believed it was on a shipping reconnaissance and eventually flew north and returned to land in Norway.

It was decided that we should fly in a pair while the third crew watched from the gallery in the ops room. On the first interception, Flt Lt Cartridge (I am sure after all this time he won't mind me referring to him as Dave) led and I was number two, a position I flew with him for many months. From first light we were on red alert, sitting in the cockpit at the end of the runway with the engines having been run up and the cockpit drill done. The first signal was the letter S for scramble and we immediately started the engines, the starter batteries were pulled away, the hatches slammed shut. A course to steer quickly followed the scramble signal. Both navigators used dead reckoning, i.e. their own calculations, at the same time as having to receive and decode the signals. It was essential that dead reckoning was used although there was no time to take any drifts which could cause large errors with the winds in the Bay of Biscay. If the first aircraft's wireless packed in for any reason, the second aircraft was to immediately take over.

As we left the Cornish coast we were given the signal A 180 (Angels 18,000). We flew into 10/10 cloud at about 4,000 feet and I immediately went line astern as I felt happier with number one's tail close to my screen than trying to keep wing-tip to wing-tip in the cloud. After a few minutes we found ourselves south of Brest with no new signal to alter course. We realised that things were not right and had no alternative but to abort the interception. Our landfall was a long way from Cornwall, just west of Portsmouth.

Back at base an inquest was held. It appeared that we had remained clearly visible on the radar screen but after reaching about 14,000 feet W/T contact had been lost. Both navigators confirmed their receivers were working, having tested them back at base. Looking at the plotting of our attempted interception it could only be described as pitiful, on our abortion we had been about 80 or 90 miles east of the bandit. However some important points were learnt. We decided to fly wing-tip to wing-tip in future to enable the navigators to see each other. They would then be able to combine their plotting by using sign language to pass over information. The crew who had remained in the ops room also suggested that a few seconds could be saved by the wireless cabin 'sparks' controller and the WAAFs moving the models on the ops table, being linked by earphones. This would make a difference of some five miles in the interception.

The next day Dave stayed behind in the ops room and I led the other crew. Exactly the same thing happened again. When we got to above 14,000 feet we lost contact. This time the navigators took the temperature as we climbed as one suggestion was that the cold could be affecting the Marconis. We were again forced to abort although at least this time Hutch made a much better landfall, despite the poor visibility. The variable weather in the Bay of Biscay in autumn certainly did not help our interception efforts and I well remember one particular trip when the weather nearly spelt disaster for us.

I was number two to Dave and we were on the way back from a failed interception. On the way out we had climbed through about 7,000 feet of cloud to come out at 18,000 feet into brilliant sunshine. On being recalled we were given a weather report that cloud base at Portreath was down to 200 feet with heavy rain. No alternative aerodrome was suggested, however, so we started slowly descending, coming into the cloud again at 16,000 feet. At 5,000 feet we found ourselves still in this black cloud. I kept my wing-tip within three feet of Dave's as I knew it would be highly dangerous to get back into formation should I lose him. At 500 feet we were still surrounded by cloud and we were now too low for us to get a bearing from the radar. At 200 feet the cloud broke and we could see the sea but the forward visibility was extremely poor with heavy rain. We continued on the last home course we had been given by Portreath but after 25 minutes Hutch called to say by his reckoning we had overshot Land's End and were headed out into the Atlantic.

After ten minutes Ossie, Dave's navigator, signalled to Hutch that he was going to turn onto a northerly course for 15 minutes followed by an easterly one with the hope that it would take us to the north-west coast of Cornwall. We started out as he had directed but after half an hour on the easterly course I could see that Dave and Ossie were having a serious discussion. Out of the corner of my eye I then noticed Ossie signalling to Hutch and could tell by the broad smile on his face that he was more or less lost. Dave was obviously thinking the same as myself that as we were having to fly at 100 feet to keep below the cloud, once we did hit land we would be below cliff level. He now signalled to me that we were going to go back up through the cloud. No way was I going to fly in formation through that lot again with the high risk of losing each other, an action which would be most dangerous. I quickly called Hutch and asked if he had any idea where we were. He said he certainly thought he could give it a go so I disobeyed Dave's order, even though I knew it could be a chargeable offence. Hutch gave me a slight variation of course and after a few minutes the coastline suddenly appeared only a few hundred yards away. There were high cliffs to the left and a coastal village straight ahead. I was just able to pull up to about 150 feet to fly over the houses and to my astonishment I saw it was Portreath village. The airfield was just to the port side, on top of the cliffs. I dared not do a proper circuit and approach in case I lost sight of it, so I performed a real split-arse half circuit at 150 feet and found it very hard to reduce speed to lower the undercart and flaps.

Having landed in a most ungainly fashion, we made our way to the ops room for the inquest. Nothing had been heard of Dave and the controller told us to go to lunch and he would ring the crew room as soon as any news came through. I went back to the aircraft and checked my tanks; as far as I could estimate they would not last beyond midday. Neither Hutch nor myself felt much like eating, we really couldn't believe this could happen to Dave and Ossie. At 1400 hours we were waiting in the crew room when news came through that they had landed safely at Thorney Island, almost 200 miles away. The weather was fast clearing and sure enough in the late afternoon they arrived back at Portreath.

Delighted that they were safe, I knew that I would still have to appear before Dave and receive either a charge or a reprimand. When I was called to his office I explained that I felt I would have been more of a hazard to him if I had followed him into the cloud, where a collision could easily have occurred, than if we split off on our own. He listened and then delivered a short lecture on disobeying orders before dismissing me. As I reached the door he called, 'Oh and Smudge, I'll pick you all up at the Sergeants Mess at seven o'clock as usual.'

We never mentioned the incident again but I knew that I had been right to do what I did and that Dave agreed with me, although protocol prevented him saying so. Ossie later filled us in on their journey. They had finally got through the cloud at 17,000 feet but unable to find a break had simply steered an easterly course while Ossie tried to obtain a 'fix'. This proved impossible so they embarked on a square search and at last, after two hours and with the tanks hovering on empty they found a break in the clouds and were able to dive through it. Luckily Ossie was then able to make a pinpoint from which they found Thorney Island.

It was quite a long time before we could subdue Hutch who was happily declaring his navigational powers to be insuperable! I know however that there would have been no joyful bragging if

Dave and Ossie had not returned. Not only was Dave a most popular Flt Lt but Maurice Osborne was a much loved character. Being 37, Ossie was the daddy of the squadron who took great delight in treating us 20-year-olds as kids. In civilian life he had been an inventor and travelled the world. He professed very strong left-wing views, even sporting a Stalin-like moustache, and celebrated madly whenever the Russians procured a victory. Nobody was ever quite sure how much of this political fervour was for real and how much was a big joke on Ossie's part but we all really enjoyed his company, even though he often had to borrow money for the beer kitty! Ossie managed to complete his tour and was awarded the Distinguished Flying Cross before being given a desk job. At the age of 39 he applied to go back on the squadron, only to be told that there were no vacancies for grandfathers.

Following all the problems of the first two interception attempts it was decided that two new tactics should be introduced. The first of these was that instead of scrambling from Portreath we should take off just before first light so as to be 40 miles out on the French coast, just south of Brest, at dawn. The second tactic, at my suggestion, was that we fly singly on interception for the simple reason that should we be split up, two blips on the radar screen would be most confusing for the controller.

That night over a beer, Hutch proclaimed he was instigating a mutiny among the navigators to protest at the extra work the single navigator would have. They would no longer be able to look for assistance from the second aircraft and Hutch thought it typical of a pilot to suggest the scheme. We pilots agreed that navigators were overpaid anyway and the evening turned into a good-humoured slanging match.

We were grounded for two days while new heaters were installed to blow hot air over the receivers and transmitters. This greatly improved their performance and gave us some small consolation that at least one of our problems had been sorted out.

Once we resumed our interception attempts we quickly discovered that there was no point trying to chase the Milk Train out into the Atlantic. Once we had missed the first time the control room would start giving us all sorts of courses, vectors and heights but to no avail. We would be left orbiting the French coast at 20,000 feet for what seemed like hours but was probably about 30 minutes. Slowly orbiting just after first light felt very lonely. We did not use the intercom except to pass messages and the Hercules engines at minimum power hardly made a whisper. It always seemed eerie to me, especially if there was 10/10 cloud below, just circling with no feeling of speed. When flying at sea level, the constant rush of passing landscape provided excitement but up here there was nothing to focus the mind on, apart from worries as to where the wind was blowing us. As soon as the 'hunt' began, such feelings were quickly forgotten. A couple of times we were left vulnerable to shore guns and interception by the Focke Wulf 190, against whom we could not hold our own. It was with great relief on these occasions that we received the controller's message to move off on a westerly course.

After almost a month with no positive results to show, morale was very low at Portreath. The idea still seemed sound but the radar was just not accurate enough at a distance of 200 to 250 miles and LRI looked doomed. The powers that be were still keen to make it work however and it was decided at group level to send three radar and wireless boffins from the Air Ministry to help us out.

The first thing the boffins made us do was fly a five-hour calibration trip in a circle of a 150-mile radius of Portreath. Dave did the eastern half, taking him to the French coast and I went out into the Atlantic, flying back right across southern Ireland from west to east. We were briefed to fly at a constant speed of 200 knots with the morse key tied down at 1,500 feet. Before we left I questioned the procedure for flying across neutral territory and was told that I would not be challenged. There were no guns in southern Ireland and the few biplanes they possessed could never get airborne in time to see which way I had gone. The afternoon was almost cloudless and I can only describe the trip across southern Ireland as enchanting. Everything looked so green and peaceful, exactly as an early autumn day should be. I felt acutely aware that down below me the people lived without the fear of war and I could not help but wonder when we would know that tranquil bliss again.

Having obtained the information they needed from our calibration trip, the boffins than proceeded to strip our aircraft receivers and transmitters in their efforts to understand the faults.

After this we took it in turns to operate while they monitored us. It was imperative that both the radar controller and the pilot kept a perfect compass course as half a degree out for a minute could jeopardise the whole interception. Hutch always took great delight in calling me up if I deviated slightly from the compass course he had given me.

About a week after the experts' arrival I was taking my turn and was surprised that soon after take-off the controller started giving orders and adjustments to course. It was obvious that today we were not just going to orbit the French coast. We were sent up to 18,000 feet and then the controller announced 'Bandit 300'. About a minute later I saw a pinhead showing up against the cloud, heading into the Atlantic. Unsure as to whether it wasn't just a fly on the windscreen, I closed in before being able to call to Hutch to transmit the long-awaited signal 'Tally Ho'.

The aircraft was a HE 111 flying just 1,000 feet below me and with the adrenaline running high, I rushed into attack and fired two short bursts before the gunners returned fire. I immediately pressed the 'tit', giving longer bursts and as I broke to starboard I could see that both of his engines were pouring smoke. My opponent quickly disappeared into the cloud and I headed down after him, descending through 5,000 feet of cloud. There was no sign of him on the other side. I then dipped to 1,000 feet but could see only the choppy sea. Eventually Hutch agreed to call for a course for home.

Our reception was overwhelmingly enthuasiatic, the fact that we had shot down an enemy aircraft having to take second place to the fact that we had proved that long-range interception could work. Our efforts were considered to be a perfect interception with no jinking about and last minute alterations of course or height.

That night the Portreath pub saw a grand celebration with everybody who had been involved in the project delighted at its success. I was probably the one who harboured some doubts. Could it have been more luck than judgement? After all when I first saw the aircraft it was only a pinhead in a vast sky and could have been five miles away. However my doubts were dismissed by the boffins who insisted that statistics from the Battle of Britain proved that a single aircraft could not have been seen if over two and a half miles away.

Having been thus reassured as to the success of the project I lost no time in joining the celebrations wholeheartedly especially once we heard that a German wireless station had been unable to contact the HE 111. Both Hutch and I felt that we had struck an important double towards the war effort, especially when our controller let slip that if there had been no improvement in interception within the week the project had been due to shut down. We would have returned to the squadron and the wireless cabin would have been dismantled.

Fired up by success we all eagerly awaited another interception to confirm that we really were on the right tracks. Two days later Dave proved that the method worked but it was far from a happy event. Watching from the ops room his course seemed to be good with few alterations and indeed just as the models on the table were moved to show an interception, the magic 'Tally Ho' came through, causing whoops of joy in the ops room. The plots then began to show Dave coming back which seemed strange as he was not in contact with Portreath and would normally have been asking for courses home. However we went to Dispersal to wait for his arrival and what we hoped would be good news.

After about an hour and a half the aircraft landed and we could tell by Dave and Ossie's faces that something was seriously wrong. Both men looked quite distraught as they climbed into Dave's van and headed for the ops room.

Almost three hours later they came out, Dave going straight to his office leaving Ossie to come over to the crew room and tell their sad tale. Their 'successful' interception had turned out to be on a Blenheim heading for the Middle East via Gibraltar. Having followed all the controller's directions, when they came upon the aircraft, Dave had dived straight down and fired a burst before recognising it as a Blenheim. Luckily they had just heard that the Blenheim had arrived safely in Gibraltar and the Wing Commander who was piloting the aircraft was not reporting the incident.

My heart really went out to Dave as I could imagine how easy it was to pounce and fire before realising the mistake. I knew from my own experience how the anticipation of the chase led to a surge of adrenaline and the automatic reaction was to fire immediately the aircraft was within range. After all, one of the main ideas behind interception was for us to have the element of surprise and be the first one to shoot.

There were various theories put forward as to what went wrong with this operation. The controller at first thought that the Blenheim was in German hands. Later it was thought that either the Blenheim's crew had accidentally switched off their FFI or that having left Portreath that morning it had been misrouted and the control room had not been informed. The fact that the Wg Cdr was not going to press for an inquiry did point the blame in the Blenheim's direction. Happily, Dave's misfortune did not spell the end for the interception programme and four days later I was able to prove that the first success had not been a fluke.

On this particular op I had just spent 40 minutes circling at 20,000 feet, with the top of the cloud at 16,000 feet, when we were given a vector and some alterations. A few minutes later I spotted a Heinkel 111 about 2,000 feet below me and almost a mile away. I immediately dived and although he managed to open fire first I gained on him firing short bursts all the while. Cowlings appeared to blow off the Heinkel and I saw the starboard engine was on fire. My opponent went into a steep dive into the cloud and I cautiously followed. Coming out the cloud, I could see no sign of him and headed for home. This hit was once again confirmed in the afternoon by the German signal stations repeatedly calling the Heinkel up with no response.

Five days later I had a near perfect interception. While orbiting at 18,000 feet I was told to vector on a westerly course and on doing so the message 'Bandit to port' came through. Sure enough there was an ME 110 just above the cloud and under one and a half miles away. I expected him to turn and fight but instead he dived for the cloud. My only chance was to hose him with fire before he reached the safety of cover. I held my thumb down on the button, allowing for a colossal deflection. Unfortunately as we were unable to see him in the cloud I was unable to claim either a hit or a miss.

That afternoon Wg Cdr Williams, who was CO of the two Polish Spitfire squadrons at Portreath, came over to our little detachment to give us a talk. To our astonishment it turned into an accusation that I had wilfully wasted valuable ammunition by 'hosepiping' the ME 110. I was furious, but being only a Sgt Pilot I had to hold my tongue. We put this uncalled for outburst down to a bit of petty jealousy as we were taking a certain amount of acclaim away from his Spits. Nine months later I found myself in the same compound as the Wg Cdr at Stalag Luft III.

The next morning Air Vice-Marshal Sir Philip Joubert paid us a visit. He gave us an informal talk in the crew room, praising our work with experimental LRI, before telling us that LRI was being introduced immediately at all coastal stations from Bircham Newton up to Sumburgh. On the conclusion of his talk, he came over to Hutch and I and asked why we thought we had been the most successful crew on interceptions so far. I considered that luck played a great part and told the Air Vice-Marshal that it could just as well have been any of the crews. Two days later however I was ordered to report to the Medical Officer for an eye check. Those on high wanted to check if there was any correlation between the ability to spot bandits at a distance and an individual's personal eyesight. It appeared that my long sight was well above average even by the RAF standards

Everybody from the LAC fitters and riggers, who had given us 100 per cent availability, to the LAC wireless operators were delighted that at last the interception project was proving such a success. Dave was made a squadron leader and we were told that three crews from the squadron at Bircham Newton were coming down to be instructed on LRI. This latter piece of news was both good and bad. Good because it meant that at last we would be able to have 24-hour passes, bad because Dave's Standard van could only take the six of us on our jaunts to the local pubs. Dave, Ossie, Hutch and myself had already voluntarily forgone two leaves that were due, being too wrapped up in the project to up and go, so we really were going to make the best of the next ones.

On our first 24 hours, Hutch and I hitched to Penzance and stayed at the Queen's Hotel. On our first night we got chatting to two sisters, the elder of whom was in the Wrens while the younger was waiting for her eighteenth birthday in order to be able to join up. Much against my principles, I was most attracted by the younger sister Eira, and went to stay at her home on my next 24-hour leave. It was an enjoyable weekend involving quite a family celebration as her father was home on leave from the Merchant

Navy where he was captain of a P & O liner, now acting as a troop carrier. I had almost forgotten what it was like to live in a family environment and I must say it made a pleasant change from camp.

Eira lived on the outskirts of Penzance and by altering course slightly on my way back from ops I would often beat up the house. On reflection this may not have been the best course of action to endear myself to her mother but nonetheless I received an invite for my next leave. Before then I was posted back to Bircham Newton but felt that I had done the right thing once I had rung her and promised to write.

The new crews who arrived at Portreath from Bircham Newton were unknown to us as we had now been away from the squadron for over three months. Of the new pilots the most surprising was an Australian, Flt Lt Rose, who had lost six inches from his left leg when baling out of a Blenheim. Although he walked with a stick it did not seem to affect his flying ability. He was a regular with the Australian Air Force sent to the squadron for operational experience to enable him to lead his own Australian squadron. Quite amazingly, Flt Lt Rose was one of the biggest snobs going, a far cry from the many other Aussies we had on the squadron. He quite obviously did not approve of Dave's friendliness towards the non-commissioned aircrew. However he relaxed slightly when he realised that our respect for Dave was in no way lessened by his warmth and Flt Lt Rose soon became the seventh body to squeeze into Dave's van of an evening.

We again started going out in pairs so as to teach the new crews the tricks of the trade and hopefully how to avoid the disappointments. Just as the crews were picking it up we were all ordered back to Bircham Newton, a sister squadron having been detailed to take over from us.

The day before we were due to leave, a week before Christmas, Dave and I were on aerodrome defence for the afternoon, the two Polish squadrons having gone on a French sweep. We were only on stand-by, not alert, which meant we could stay in the crew room and in case of emergency would only have 50 yards to run to our aircraft. I made the most of the peace and warmth in the crew room and was in the middle of a pleasant afternoon nap by the stove when I was rudely awakened by a series of eight explosions. All I could see was piles of shattered glass and thick coatings of soot as I joined the scramble into the air raid shelter. Safely inside I was just brushing the soot from my uniform when a ground crew asked why I wasn't on stand-by. Horrified, I realised that instead of being safely tucked away I should be out defending the camp! There was a great deal of good humoured sarcasm as I pushed my way back out of the shelter, guiltily having to explain my retreat as I went. Dave was already clearing the boundary fence at the end of the runway when I emerged and my ground crew were waiting by their starter trolleys, Hutch already in place with maps spread before him. I need not dwell on the torrents of tongue-in-cheek abuse I received from my navigator as he saw me come out of the shelter. No sooner had I climbed the ladder then the hatch was slammed. The cockpit drill had been completed earlier so without even waiting to belt up, I waved the fitter away, opened up straight from the dispersal point and was airborne in no time.

The bandit had a good start on us and by the time we were over Falmouth, ops room was calling us home. Luckily the only damage suffered had been the shattered windows in our dispersal offices and the annihilation of the stove chimney. This did not concern us as it would be our sister squadron, arriving the next day, who would have to make do without warmth!

11

We arrived back at the squadron to a sea of new faces. Considerable losses combined with postings to the Middle East for the desert push meant that many old friends had gone. There was a high proportion of Australians fresh to the squadron, keen to volunteer for the Middle East now Japan had joined the war and things looked so bad for their native land.

Dave was now Flight Commander for A Flight, much to everybody's approval and he showed all the keenness and determination that one would expect. Four days after our arrival, he called Hutch and I into his office and told us to pack up again as we were going to the Shetlands for Christmas, along with himself and Flt Lt Rose. The job was hush-hush and he was unable to elaborate. Sumburgh really was the last place anyone would want to spend the festive season. The whole island was dry apart from the messes where the beer was brought by boat from the mainland. Owing to the rough crossing, it could take up to a fortnight to settle and become drinkable. Two weeks seemed rather an excessive wait for a pint by any calculation! Just to add to our festive frolics, no WAAFs had ever been allowed to go to the island.

When we arrived we found three aircraft and crews from our two sister Beaufighter squadrons. The rumours were rife as to why we were there. The briefing was scheduled for the next afternoon, Christmas Eve, and in the meantime we were to make sure that our aircraft were 100 per cent available as there were no spare ones. Dave ordered us to carry out air tests the next morning. A skeleton ground staff had travelled with us, somehow managing to squeeze themselves and the toolboxes into the fuselage of the Beaus. We were delighted that Flt Sgt Jerry Jay was among our passengers as he was definitely the maintenance whiz-kid. An ex-Halton boy, Jerry was granted a commission at the beginning of 1942 and promotion quickly followed.

At the briefing we found that we were to give fighter cover for a commando raid due to land on Boxing Day at first light, along the Norwegian coast at Vaagso. The naval force would consist of the cruiser *Hastings,* supported by various destroyers and landing craft. Sqn Ldr Sam McHardy, our late Flt Cdr, would be controller on board *Hastings*. There were to be two detachments of fighter Blenheims from another two sister squadrons based at Wick, who would cover from first light to 1000 hours when the Beaus would take over and see the job completed. We were the last sortie and would take over at 1400 hours and stay until last light, by which time the naval force should be well clear of the coast.

In the early years of the war there was an unwritten understanding between the two sides that there were no air raids on Christmas Day. We had been instructed to carry out air tests however. Once I was airborne and had checked the aircraft thoroughly, I decided that as it was Christmas Day Hutch and I would have a little outing and go north to see the flying boat base at Sullom Voe. My whim satisfied, I was heading back to Sumburgh when I noticed a dirty great cold front with menacing black cloud in front. As we began to go through heavy snow and the visibility reduced rapidly, I kicked myself for not having checked the forecast with Station met before setting out. The runway at Sumburgh was right on the coastline so I decided to drop to sea level and follow the coast round, with the hope that I would see the east end of the short runway and be able to do a split-arse line-up. I had to open the bad weather panel in the side screen. I did consider flying down to the mainland where I could try to come down at Wick, but decided that for the reputation of the squadron and the need for 100 per cent availability I must get back to Sumburgh.

By looking sideways and then referring to his map, Hutch was able to make a couple of pinpoints of the rocky coast and give me

64

a shout when he thought the runway was about a mile ahead. I immediately throttled back and lowered the undercart. Catching sight of the runway out of the bad weather panel, I did a split-arse S-turn, lowered the flaps and groped my way down. We had just touched down when I saw the intersection flash past and knew that we would overshoot. I applied full brake with the control column pulled right into my stomach and fully cut the engines. As I felt the aircraft hit the sand dune I shut my eyes, knowing that only a few yards of beach and a couple of coils of barbed wire separated us from the sea. Miraculously the aircraft came to a stop and I opened my eyes to look straight down into the sea. We were perched on top of a sandbank with coils of wire looped round the propeller and wings, holding the aircraft out of a watery grave.

It was quite a job to open the hatch and squeeze out and I hardly dared look to see the damage. As we stood looking at the mess, all Hutch said was, 'What a bloody arrival,' and I inwardly had to agree with him. The blizzard was so strong that it was hard to tell but I could see that the undercart had remained intact on hitting the sand and I was delighted that there seemed to be no obvious breakage. Nobody had been able to see us so we struck off for the crew hut where we found Jerry Jay and asked him to round up all available ground crew. Half an hour later, with the help of several pairs of wire cutters, a tractor and many able bodies, my aircraft stood on the runway. I started the engines and with Jerry standing behind me we taxied to the watch office. Much to our relief there was no abnormal vibration when we ran her to maximum throttle which indicated that the props were undamaged. With the blizzard abating it was now up to the ground crew to carry out a full examination. Already feeling bad about having everybody out in such filthy weather, I sincerely hoped that this would not result in the ground crew missing their Christmas dinner.

At Christmas it was traditional in the RAF for the airmen to have their lunch served by the officers and sergeants. While we were doing our waiter act, news came through that the operation had been delayed by 24 hours. I was pleased to hear this as not only did it mean that there was more time to repair the aircraft should she require it, but we could also have a bit of a party. Later in the afternoon, Jerry came to say that apart from severe scratching, the aircraft seemed perfectly O.K. I felt most relieved and immediately called Hutch to join Jerry and I for another air test. This time I made no Christmas Day detours and was down in ten minutes.

The rest of the evening past most pleasantly. Hutch and I had been invited by Dave to join him in the Officers Mess for drinks before dinner. We reeled back to the Sergeants Mess two hours late for our meal, having celebrated Christmas in style with Dave and Flt Lt Rose, who turned out to be far from the stuffy chap we had mistaken him for. The mess had kindly kept hot food for us which we demolished before falling into bed.

On the whole, much of the war propaganda that filled the media was greeted with a proportion of disbelief by those in the forces. However there were a number of stories that seemed so convincing that we happily joined in with everyone else in believing them. One of these was that Britain was capable of invasion in December 1941. All over Christmas, rumours had buzzed that our operation was going to involve the invasion of Norway. By the end of our third briefing, an hour before take-off on the day after Boxing Day, the rumours were scotched when we were told the Commandos and the Navy were going to be looking for a heavy water plant. Heavy water plants were a requirement for nuclear fusion.

The day of ops arrived with a cloudless sky and a good forecast. We were taxiing to the end of the runway for take-off at 1200 hours when we received a red Verey light from the watch tower. A van came tearing round the perimeter fence and out jumped the Assistant Intelligence Officer who informed each of us that word had just been received that eighteen HE111 had arrived at Herdla aerodrome.

We flew in loose formation at sea level until we were within 50 miles of Vaagso where we rose to 1,000 feet to enable the Navy to identify us. Ossie brought us into a good landfall with the naval force dead ahead. The three Beaus we were relieving waggled their wings and set course for home. At the final briefing we had been told to give cover at 400 feet so that if the ships were attacked the Navy would have air space for their anti-aircraft guns. In the RAF we respected what the Navy said as they were known to shoot first and ask questions later.

On arrival we could see that the Commandos were assembling

on the quayside ready for evacuation and things seemed to be going according to plan. After about 20 minutes, Squadron Leader MacHardy suddenly came on the R/T telling us that enemy aircraft were approaching from 180 degrees at 10,000 feet. Our brief to stay at 400 feet in order to fend off a sea level attack meant that we were now well below the enemy. We individually started to climb but were still only at 6,000 feet when we spotted two loose formations of HE111s, each containing nine aircraft. We continued to climb outside the naval cone while the naval barrage began firing. We had to watch as each flight dropped their bombs and it was with great relief that we saw them fall well short of HMS *Hastings* and the destroyer escort.

As soon as the enemy had discharged their bombs they broke formation and headed quickly for home. I had expected to see a fighter escort of 110s or even 109s but there was no sign of one. As they turned they still had the advantage of about 2,000 feet on us but I picked one out, noticing as I did so that Dave and Flt Lt Rose had both done likewise. This came as no surprise as I had realised early on in the op that both pilots were gong hunting. The sky seemed full of HE111s all tearing home in shallow dives as we gave chase. I could hear Sqn Ldr MacHardy calling for us to return to continue air cover but as neither of the other two pilots seemed to be taking any notice I continued with them. As the R/T grew fainter I just picked out MacHardy's voice demanding our immediate return. The use of the word 'immediate' brought me to my senses, after all I was only a Flt Sgt and I realised I could be in for a major bollicking if I didn't obey.

Leaving Dave and Flt Lt Rose in full chase I returned to my post and was soon joined by enemy company. Two Arada seaplanes which must have been shadowing the force appeared on the horizon. Just as I was thinking about giving chase, I spotted three Ju 88s in the distance. I therefore continued my tight circling at 300 feet above the ships, unable to break it for fear of letting an intruder in. Sqn Ldr MacHardy was continually warning me of bandits in the area and as I circled I cursed Dave and Flt Ft Rose for leaving me on my own in this predicament.

Everything below seemed to be going very smoothly but after about half an hour I couldn't help but wonder if my fellow pilots were O.K. Five minutes later I saw Flt Lt Rose approaching from the south and he flashed the correct Verey lights. A few minutes later, Dave arrived back. I was extremely pleased to see them both and soon forgot the abuse I had silently poured on them.

The sun set soon after we had regrouped and *Hastings* and the destroyers began to sail full speed for home, leaving a sizeable wash as they went. The bandits stayed on the horizon until all light had gone and 15 minutes later our orders came through to return to base. Dave put his formation lights on and I tucked my wing tip a few feet from his and gave a final farewell to the force at 100 feet. It was a beautiful night for flying, clear with a full moon and I thoroughly enjoyed the hour journey back across the glittering sea. As we neared home a flashing light caught my eye which Hutch identified as a lighthouse some 70 miles away on the northern tip of the Shetlands, such was the visibility. I always felt an immense warmth towards lighthouse keepers who would light up to help us home, even though they risked becoming a target by doing so. It was a great comfort to see a welcoming light after hours of darkness.

At the debriefing we were told that the operation had been so successful that it was thought the Navy would be in safe waters by first light and we could therefore stand down. The nine Beaus operating from Sumburgh had sustained no loses although unfortunately four of the twelve Blenheims from Wick had been lost. After the usual bacon and eggs we all met up in the Officers Mess to resume our Christmas celebrations. Both Dave and Flt Lt Rose claimed a HE111 apiece, having chased them for almost 60 miles before they could get into a firing position. Hutch and I made sure they didn't forget that their success had almost left us high and dry and there was a great deal of jovial abuse on all sides that evening.

The Vaagso raid was regarded as a great success in its combination of the three forces and the Admiralty actually praised the RAF for its role, a most unusual source of praise indeed. The next day we returned to Bircham Newton to find that both A for Angela and Dave's R for Roberta were to be sent to the Middle East and we were to receive the new mark of Beau. The chief improvement on these was the belt feed for the cannons so Hutch

68

was naturally delighted. The old feed involved the navigator bending almost double to unclip the empty drums, remove them, unstrap the full drums and clip them into position. This was torturous work and almost impossible unless the aircraft was flying straight and level. God knows why all Beau navigators didn't suffer from slipped discs.

I had more or less unpacked my suitcase and reacquainted myself with Bircham Newton when I was woken at 0300 hours one morning by the dispatching sergeant and told to report to the ops room immediately. As we raced across the aerodrome I noted with dismay the atrocious weather conditions. Alternate rain and sleet beat down on the truck's roof. The controller's orders were short and concise. We were to get down to St. Eval as soon as possible, packing just a toothbrush and razor. Although the controller refused to elaborate I knew from talking to some of the chaps on our sister squadrons that St. Eval spelt bad news.

A daily reconnaissance flight was operated by the Photo Reconnaissance Unit (PRU) out of St. Eval. They were using stripped-down Spits, carrying only a pilot and camera to obtain information on the *Scharnhorst* and *Gneisenau* warships. This was quite feasible on clear days when the aircraft could keep a height of 24,000 feet, well clear of anti-aircraft guns and enemy fighters. However, when there was cloud cover or the French underground reports were doubtful, the Air Ministry, under pressure from the Navy, had started to send Beaus in at sea level. Out of seven attempts only one aircraft had returned home. The question that puzzled me was why 19 Group were calling for a single aircraft from 400 miles away when their own Beaus were at Carew Cheriton in South Wales.

Immediately after take-off we hit heavy rain and sleet but the met had advised us that we should be through it in about 40 minutes so I decided to fly at 2,000 feet, confident that we would be out of the weather front before daylight. After almost 90 minutes dawn was just breaking and I gradually began to lower the aircraft, wanting to get below the cloud before we reached any high ground. Thankfully we broke cloud at 800 feet and it was now a matter of finding an aerodrome where we could land and obtain a new weather report to help us on our way.

Hutch was unable to recognise any pinpoints so we started a

square search. Twenty minutes later we spotted an airfield under the starboard wing and landed to find we were at Abingdon FTS. The station weatherman seemed at a bit of a loss having to deal with an operational crew but the control tower finally got through to 19 Group. They informed us that the weather was still bad between Abingdon and St. Eval and advised a new route taking us round the front. This involved flying almost to the French coast and then returning to Falmouth. We eventually arrived at St. Eval at midday with cloud at 800 feet although the rain had stopped. The journey had certainly given me plenty of time to think about what lay ahead of us.

Brest harbour and the surrounding area was the most heavily fortified part of Europe. I knew that all the disastrous sea-level reconnaissances had been carried out flying west to east which meant that at the end of the 20-mile stretch there was no alternative but to turn and more or less follow the same path back. Travelling at sea level, this made the aircraft an easy target especially over the heaviest stretch of fire from Ouessant onwards.

I wanted to explore the possibility of hitting the coast ten miles north of Brest before climbing into 10/10 cloud at 1,000 to 1,500 feet. I felt we could then fly an easterly course followed by a southerly one on Hutch's dead reckoning and then, with luck, break cloud when the dead reckoning position put us a mile or two east of Brest. This should bring the river and harbour under the starboard wing and enable us to turn west and dive with all power. We would then have maximum speed and would have a much better chance of clearing the gauntlet of guns. We had no option but to chance the balloon defences.

Before we reported to the ops room, I quickly put my idea to Hutch who felt it had definite possibilities. After all, we agreed, surely it was better to try something new after so many failures. Unfortunately the controller was a wingless wonder. He chastised us for not arriving earlier before casually mentioning that we would be doing a reconnaissance of Brest harbour. Infuriated by his manner, I told him we needed half an hour to sort our route out. Hutch and I carefully ran through my plan, and, deciding there were few flaws, returned to put the idea to the controller. He dismissed the whole scheme, maintaining that we had to go the same route as the previous attempts.

I suddenly saw red. Here we were, cut off from our squadron, under a different group we weren't even attached to, being told by some unknown controller that we must fly a path that would most probably result in us being shot down. Although I was keen to do my part for my country I certainly did not intend to be unnecessary cannon fodder and I demanded to speak to the controlling officer of the group. A phone was handed to me, thankfully this officer was much more ready to listen to us and after a thorough look at our courses, agreed to let us try. He realised that by approaching from the east we would only have ten miles of defence to fly through before we got to Ouessant by which time we hoped to have built up an airspeed of over 300 miles an hour. We were also helped by the fact that the met forecast 10/10 cloud at 1,200 feet along the French coast that very afternoon. The PRU had been unable to photograph the battleships for the past 48 hours and intelligence were crying out for more information.

We were given photographs to study and memorise by intelligence and then it was up to us. Neither Hutch nor myself spoke much as the crew van took us to dispersal point; we really were going to need every ounce of luck. I felt much better however when the new A for Angela's two engines were whirring and I was taxiing to the end of the runway. Just as I turned for take-off I was stopped by a red Verey light from the watch tower. The next thing I saw was the Station Commander speeding in his Humber brake along the perimeter fence, heading for our aircraft. On jumping out, he came straight over, opened the hatch and climbed up the ladder behind me. His orders were that on no account was I to go ahead if the cloud cover was not 10/10 and below 1,500 feet. He then jumped down and went in front to give me the O.K. for take-off. It did seem strange to look down on the cap bedecked with scrambled egg instead of the usual scruffy cap waved by an AC 2.

We had only gone 20 miles from the English coast when I saw that the met had got it wrong. The cloud was already breaking up. We continued to fly at sea level until we were about 15 miles from the French coast and it was time to start our climb. I could tell that the cloud was far higher than 1,500 feet and indeed we were still climbing for cloud cover at 3,500 feet. All we could see were pretty little cotton wool puffs from the enemy coastal guns, useless for providing cover. With our hopes of surprise gone, we turned in a steep dive and headed for home, before the fighters found us.

After debriefing we were told we were to remain on 24-hour stand-by and go no further afield than the Mess and our billets. The PRU were able to obtain their pictures the next day and for three days we just waited. The huge risk involved in the operation seemed to magnify with each hour that past. Every time I heard the tannoy switch on, my stomach seemed to hit my mouth. For me all RAF tannoys had a foreboding sound, even the most glamorous WAAF couldn't make them sound friendly, but the one at St. Eval seemed worse than any. Hutch and I just hung around the Mess, glancing at magazines. There was always a wide selection of books available but I never remember seeing any aircrew engrossed in reading and this was certainly not a time to start. Each time we crossed from our billet to the Mess we could see A for Angela standing at dispersal with her nose held high.

On the fourth day neither of us felt we could take much more of the waiting, so I suggested that the aircraft should have its engines run and airtested. It was agreed that we should take her up and also that we could put in some practice on our intended tactic. It was a great relief to be flying again and we immediately headed for Padstow where we had decided to carry out our practice. As the weather was exactly opposite to what we should want, with cloud being about 4/10 at well over 2,000 feet, I kept my head down, staring at the banks of instruments, so that we could try to reach our target by dead reckoning. We went out to sea for 20 miles and came back in 8 miles north of Padstow. I tried not to cheat by looking up and we did improve on each of our three runs but it was far from perfect.

We remained on stand-by for another four days. The weather over Brest thankfully stayed clear and the PRU were able to obtain all the pictures they needed. When the order came for us to return to Bircham Newton, you couldn't see us for dust. We arrived back just in time to take leave, having forgone two lots since the summer. The tension of the last few days was greatly relieved by a few nights in London enjoyed by Hutch, myself and an Australian crew. I then headed back to Thorney to see my family.

Left: Martin, 1938.

I was somewhat surprised when I was recently sent the picture and caption shown below. Hutch is standing on my right.

Below: **BEAU MEN. Squadron Ledader D L Cartridge, DFC (holding pet dog) and some of the crews of 248 Squadron, pictured at Portreath airfield. Flt Sgt Smith (extreme rt, back row) was tragically killed in an air collision on return to base after a strike./G Medcalf**

A for Angela. Dyce, 1942.

Stalag Luft III, 1944. Frank Lowe (Red) third from right, myself extreme right.

Last fence, Fitzwilliam Point-to-Point, 1959. Very tired horse and jockey.

Hindoy. The isolated island where Hutch and I were finally washed up, 19 July 1942.

Hindoy. Drinking from the same puddle in May 1995 as I drank from 53 years before.

1995. Hjordis Spord who courageously fed and sheltered Hutch and myself on our arrival on Hindoy in 1942.

Liberation Service, May 1995, Vaerlandet, Norway. Left to right: Frank Lowe, DFM, Group Captain Christopher Granville-White, CBE and myself.

12

There was a great deal of commotion on our return to the squadron as the *Scharnhorst* and *Gneisenau* were expected to make a dash from Brest harbour at any time. The squadron were keeping a continuous surveillance of the Dutch and German coasts. It was most important during these reconnaissance trips to return to base as soon as possible with information and not court trouble. However, I couldn't resist 'having a go' on one occasion when I caught sight of two ships travelling close to shore during daylight. I figured they must have a pretty important cargo to be out when it was light so I got between the shore and my target and turned so as to attack broadside. I thought the smaller ship was possibly the flak ship and it was the larger one that I aimed for. I set my sights on the bridge and saw it take the full force of my guns. The belt-fed cannons meant that I could keep my finger on the button confident that we would not run out of drums. Hutch said that the guns of the flak ship were falling well behind us as I had given Angela full throttle.

The day after this encounter all hell let loose as the *Scharnhorst* and *Gneisenau* had slipped through the Straits of Dover. By 1300 hours the whole squadron was on immediate readiness although by nightfall we still had not been called upon. Next morning we were ordered to pack up and fly to Dyce from where we were to start continuous recces of the Norwegian coast. On the second day at Dyce the squadron flew down to Leuchars to pick up a squadron of Torpedo Beauforts and escort them down the Norwegian coast as there was a strong possibility that the *Scharnhorst* and *Gneisenau* would make a break for the Atlantic by using the very northerly route.

The CO was actually leading the squadron, the first operation he had been part of for some time. I was flying number two to Dave

73

as we set off to arrive just south of Bergen and then continue south, down to the Skagerrak. The idea was to ensure the Beauforts had maximum cover for as long as we possibly could. The Beauforts had seven hours endurance to our five-and-a-half but flying at 160 knots was well below our normal cruising speed and we hoped to stay with them almost to the end.

I had just estimated that there would be another three-quarters of an hour flying when to my amazement the CO broke formation and signalled for the squadron to return home. Closing up on Dave, he gestured to his gauges to indicate that, like me, he had ample fuel for another 45 minutes. The CO was far from well thought of and I knew that Dave was in two minds as to whether to obey him. Indeed most of us were struggling with our consciences, feeling terrible about abandoning the Beauforts before it was necessary. In the end a very straggly A Flight followed their leader and headed back to base. We were to return to base individually as the last hour would be in darkness. I felt ashamed to be heading for home and knew that Hutch was equally worried. Apart from asking me for the fuel tank reading and calling over the courses, he didn't speak on the journey back.

It was more like a funeral parlour than an ops room as we assembled for debriefing, all waiting to see what the CO had to say for himself. In fact he never turned up, leaving Dave to more or less take over. Dave's feelings were only too evident and it was a much dispirited party that sat down to bacon and eggs. Quite a crowd seemed to gather in my billet that evening, mulling over the mortification of our withdrawal. At midnight the dispatching sergeant appeared to tell us to report for ops at 0300 hours. It hardly seemed worth going to bed so we made our way to the Sergeants Mess and dozed in chairs. Outside it was snowing heavily and the snow ploughs were on the runway clearing a path.

On reporting to the ops room we all drew a sigh of relief on learning that the Beauforts had returned safely to Leuchars, having encountered no shipping force and, more importantly to us, no enemy aircraft. The CO was never seen again and nobody minded. Within a week we had a new CO, Wg Cdr Pike, a brilliant chap who had been awarded the DSO and DFC. He made a point of quickly getting to know us all and was usually the first to lead.

As the Beauforts had not encountered the enemy force south of Bergen and in the Skagerrak, we were briefed that night to search the coast northwards. Ten of us were to take off at one minute intervals, timed to arrive on the Norwegian coast from first light onwards. The take-off was a total disaster. I was due to take-off second, after Dave. The ground crew had been unable to sweep the snow off all ten aircraft and some aircrew were scurrying around in the dark trying to do this themselves. As I groped my way from dispersal onto the perimeter track I found that another aircraft had got stuck across the track. I waited for as long as I could for him to be removed but with my engines starting to heat up I realised that I would have to get Angela moving. Switching on my landing light, I ran off the perimeter and went round the aircraft making my way to the flare-path. By this time the order of take-off had gone to the wall and it was a case of grabbing a green light when it came on and hoping nobody else was in the way. The snow ploughs had only been able to clear a third of the width of the runway so to add to the complications we were taking off between massive banks of snow.

I was even more relieved than normal to be up and away and was glad that after an hour's flying I was able to come down to 200 feet and then later on to sea level. Twenty miles from the Norwegian coast we could see the shore guns and flak lighting up the dawn twilight. Just as we completed our stretch I spotted two 109s and three 110s flying across my beam at about 500 feet. This was the last thing I felt like at the end of a traumatic night and I quickly turned to port and headed for home on full throttle. Hutch gave a course to steer and told me we'd been spotted and were being chased. Luckily we had a good start on them and they were unable to close the gap, soon giving up, possibly because they were short of fuel.

At this stage I would just like to say that there was one thing Hutch and I disagreed on and that was smoking in the aircraft. When we were safely on our way home, Hutch would always light a cigarette, an action which annoyed me intensely. I found that my senses were always heightened when flying and the slightest change of noise or smell would start alarm bells ringing in my head. Even with the bulletproof doors on the fuselage closed, I could smell the match as he lit up. Knowing my disapproval he would never call up to say he was going to smoke and invariably on smelling the sulphur, I would ask, 'Are you smoking?' to which I would always get a curt 'Yes'. A pipe-smoker myself, I did not condemn him on health reasons, it just seemed as if there were enough fire hazards on an aircraft, especially with the constant smell of dope, fuel and guns, without lighting up a cigarette.

We were now constantly patrolling the Norwegian coast in case the German naval force made a break for the Atlantic. This would be comparatively easy for the *Scharnhorst* and *Gneisenau* with the deep water and many islands for cover. Combined with this we also provided escorts for the Russian convoys. We carried out these escort patrols in pairs, I was always number two to Dave, and they were not the most exciting of ops. The weather always seemed bad and the ops room positioning of the ships seemed somewhat haphazard giving inaccurate rendezvous points. This was hardly surprising, given that there was total radio silence combined with the bad weather, making even a massive naval force hard to pinpoint in such a vast expanse of sea. I remember twice having to carry out a square search which naturally cut down on the amount of time we could cover the force. Once they had passed out of our limit of endurance, they had many hundreds of miles to travel without cover, totally open to air attack.

On one of these escorts I managed to do five-and-a-half hours endurance and only just made it home, hitting the Shetlands from a northerly direction and relying on the lighthouses to help tune my position.

Our maritime escort and reconnaissance duties were briefly interrupted by the need to provide an escort for some Hampdens, recently fitted to carry torpedoes. They were based at Leuchars and we were required to rendezvous off the coast in the Moray Firth for a training exercise. This was a total shambles. We initially tried to position ourselves with the Hampdens flying at 600 feet. Weighed down by the external torpedoes, the Hampdens were unable to maintain much speed and we simply overshot them. At the next attempt I put on about 10 degrees of flap but even then was only just above stalling speed and once again had to drop away to save myself. Eventually we went into a very loose formation and managed to stay with the other aircraft for about an hour. Safe when flying straight, even this was dicey when it came to turning. Had we gone down to sea level, the height we would have had to use in operations, the task would have been highly dangerous. On returning to base we agreed that our only means of escort could be if we circled the Hampdens, although this would put our fuel consumption right up.

It was about this time that long-range interception was introduced at Dyce and Sumburgh. There was still only a handful of us who were familiar with this technique, so we found ourselves teaching the other squadron crews. Many of the old problems reared their ugly heads again but we were better able to deal with them now. It was a matter of keeping a suitcase constantly packed as we were always being shunted from station to station to carry out operations. How we all dreaded going to Sumburgh, with its shaken-up beer and lack of social life. I well remember one time up there when we received orders to be back at Dyce for 1600 hours. A bet went round as to who would be the first crew in the Caledonian, our watering hole in Aberdeen, that evening.

I was carrying seven ground crew and their toolboxes, but determined to win, I had an idea for saving five minutes. I told the ground crew to load everything including the chocks while I ran the engines up on the brakes. This meant that I could only give them half throttle as the brakes would not hold for any longer and it was a technique that was strictly against rules. We were taking off on the long runway, from south-west to north-east which meant we had to be airborne quickly to prevent colliding with the buildings about 50 yards from the far end. We were clearing the runway, at the crucial stage when maximum power was needed, when the port engine faltered. I felt Angela loose height and for a few horrific moments thought that I was going to plough through the Sergeants Mess, taking seven ground crew with me. To my immense relief the engine picked up and we scraped over the top of the mess.

Hutch and I arrived in the Cally first that night and claimed our free pints but I had certainly been taught a lesson. It did not pay to break aviation rules. If I had run the engines up properly, the condensation in the carburettors would have been cleared and we would have had no problem.

13

A few weeks later we were using Wick and enjoying a drink one evening, when the Orderly Room Sergeant came in and told Hutch and myself that news had just come through that we were mentioned in Despatches. After the congratulations, I bought a round and a party developed. I knew I had been recommended for the DFM and although I made an outward show of delight I was somewhat disappointed. It was all very well being mentioned but I wanted to actually gain the award. I did not relish the fact but I had become something of a gong hunter and I could only wonder how much more I was expected to do before my achievements were rewarded. I was also feeling rather low at this point because things had not been going as well as I had hoped. I felt that the recces I was undertaking were often fruitless and I was still annoyed by the aborted Brest affair. My skill with long-range interception seemed to have deserted me and altogether I was feeling pretty frustrated with my performance.

In April, Bomber Command sent a couple of squadrons of four-engine bombers on a raid to destroy a heavy water plant between Herdla and Trondheim. Six Beaus were required to strafe Herdla and Trondheim aerodromes in order to keep the night fighters grounded. Trondheim was very much a borderline destination for the Beaus' endurance, in fact our northern reconnaissance always finished south of the town. Both aerodromes were also fairly difficult to approach having a natural defence by their geographical location among cliffs and mountains.

When we arrived in the ops room we saw that Wg Cdr Pike and Dave had taken the trip to go to Trondheim leaving four of us to go to Herdla. I am sure Group Headquarters did not know that Dave and the CO were both going to Trondheim. If anything were to go wrong on that raid, not only with the strafing but with the ability to return to base, there would be no outstanding leaders left on the squadron.

I was to fly number two to Flt Lt Phil Graham and of all things each group was to fly at night in formation and to strafe at the same time. This meant almost two hours of formating in the dark so it was easier to fly line astern which gave us three lots of formation lights as well as the dull red glow of the exhaust baffles. By the time we reached the Norwegian coast I could see little blue lights everywhere and the sweat was pouring off me even though I was only in battledress and shoes. The landfall was not dead accurate and Flt Lt Graham started jinking about on different courses. I pitied the poor chap acting as number four. Flying in formation is something akin to throwing a stone into a pool of water. Just as the ripples became larger further away from the centre so a slight alteration to course by the leader becomes a major deviation for those lower down the line.

After a short time Hutch pinpointed us and warned me that Herdla was coming up on the starboard side. Sure enough we were soon met with the full force of the German defences and the leader called 'Break' enabling us all to fire individually. The whole aerodrome was alight with fire and all I could see were dispersal points from where the guns were firing so I took a line straight down them with my guns firing constantly. As it turned out all four of us were attacking at the same time but this worked well and we returned to base not being able to claim any aircraft destroyed on the ground but certain that we had kept them from taking-off. I felt a lot happier that I had again been part of a successful mission.

After debriefing we hung around the ops room waiting for news of the CO and Dave who were due back an hour after us. We heard that Dave was back before going over to the mess. Although we lingered over the bacon and eggs, no news was received of Wg Cdr Pike and we knew that there was little hope for him, fuel being as low as it must have been. Ossie said they had stayed together until they found Trondheim airfield where they broke up and strafed individually. It was a great loss to the squadron as during the six weeks he had been with us Wg Cdr Pike's enthusiasm had been most infectious and we had all warmed to him.

When we returned to Dyce, Hutch and I were posted for a three-day gunnery and air-firing course at Leuchars, much to Hutch's delight as he came from Dundee. It was on this course that I very nearly wrote Angela off, totally through my own stupidity. On the squadron the aircraft's tanks were filled as soon as we had landed and a bowser was free. Unbeknown to me, at the Air Firing School the tanks were only filled at the end of the day. On our first day we flew twice in the morning and were due to go out twice again in the afternoon. After lunch I did my cockpit drill and as I finished one check I pushed the button on the fuel gauge at the same time. I was so used to the tanks being full that I failed to notice that the needle for the outer tank stayed at about the ten-gallon mark and did not go round to full.

I had been asked to take up an Air Corps youngster for flight experience and once he was standing behind me, we took off. I got in a couple of air-to-ground dives and was just about to half roll again onto the target when I sensed my passenger had left his place. Glancing behind, I saw him lying in the well being violently sick. At the same moment my port engine cut out. Although I glanced over the gauges, I still failed to see the true reading for the fuel quantity and could only think that I must get back to Leuchars immediately. Hutch let off some red Verey cartridges to warn the watch tower that it was an emergency and I prepared for a single-engine landing. The runway was clear and I was just congratulating myself on my final approach where I had plenty of height in hand, when the second engine cut out. We began to drop like a stone and the low hedge surrounding the airfield which had previously seemed so close suddenly seemed miles away. I just managed to coax Angela over the hedge and landed with a terrific thump, short of the runway. Somehow the undercart stood up to the next few seconds running across ground pitted with rabbit holes until we came to an ignoble halt.

Hutch lost no time in telling me what a bloody arrival it was as we half-lifted, half-dragged the poor Air Corps boy from the aircraft. He revived slightly on returning to terra firma and I headed off to give the duty sergeant a piece of my mind. How could he profess to maintain aircraft when this happened?

We hadn't been back in the crew room long when I saw both Angela's engines running and I went out to talk to the duty sergeant. He had great pleasure in telling me both outer fuel tanks had been empty and suggesting that perhaps I check them another time. It really was a case of familiarity breeding contempt and I was forced to eat humble pie with the duty sergeant and the ground crew.

Feeling very foolish I then went off in search of my passenger, who I discovered still looking very green. I certainly didn't help his dilemma by informing him that it was an unwritten rule that if anyone was sick it was up to them to clean up the aircraft. I did take pity on the poor chap though when he asked me if I thought he would still make aircrew. I told him that I had been a bit rough on him by half rolling and then subjecting him to the fuel drama and that sometimes air sickness happened on the first occasion and then was never felt again. I bet he wished he'd picked anyone but me to fly with that day!

The three nights we were at Leuchars were all spent in Dundee. On the first night I joined Hutch at his parents' home. The Hutchinsons were a lovely family and Hutch was clearly worshiped by his teenage sister. I was really glad to have met them and even more so three years later when I visited them in very different circumstances.

On the second night, Hutch insisted we went to see the Dundee Repertory Company. Not being a great culture buff I agreed but was somewhat worried that the show did not end until after closing time. Undeterred Hutch led me to a nearby pub where we went into a back room. After a few minutes members of the cast started to arrive, all of whom Hutch seemed to know, which was hardly surprising when he suddenly introduced his girlfriend from among them. I knew that Hutch had received fairly frequent letters from Dundee but had never suspected he had a regular girlfriend. I was delighted to meet her and also pleased that Hutch had kept her a secret. With no disrespect to such a lovely girl, I knew that Hutch felt as I did, that to survive flying we had to be 100 per cent committed to the squadron and to our crew; there just wasn't space for emotions and outside ties. We had a wonderful party that night which continued the following evening after Hutch and I had dined with his parents in town. It was well into the early hours before Hutch returned to our billet.

I was just packing up the next morning, feeling pleased with my course assessment of very good for all types of air-firing, when I witnessed a most spectacular crash. A Hurricane came over the far end of the runway at about 500 feet and was obviously trying to land. He touched down three quarters of the way down the runway and when he realised he wasn't going to have enough tarmac, he pulled his undercart up and skidded along on his belly, right into the dispersal point for the Hampdens. He hit the first Hampden with his wing and then started to spin like a top before cutting the undercarts of two more. Eventually the Hurricane came to a complete stop and out jumped a sergeant pilot from OTU, totally unscathed. He had simply panicked when his engine failed.

On arriving back at Dyce, Dave called me into his office and told me that a posting had come through for two pilots to go to Air Firing School down at Sutton Bridge on rest. As I was now the second most senior with regard to ops hours, I was selected. I did not want to go and said that I would like to stay with the squadron until I had completed a full tour, (I had nearly 30 hours still to do). Dave eventually agreed to send a married officer who was next on the list but told me it was time I was recommended for a commission and he was going to put me forward. I half-heartedly agreed, although I hoped the good life as a sergeant with its lack of worry would continue for some time. The real reason I did not want to leave the squadron at this stage was because I could not feel satisfied unless I left with a DFM. I felt that I was on course for receiving one and I did not wish to face the next generation of pilots as an instructor, without having accomplished this ambition.

Two weeks after this chat with Dave, Ossie and I went down to Edinburgh for our medical and interviews, enjoying a good night out at the North British on the way. I seemed now to be doing more and more long-range interception and I felt that Dave was spinning my 30 hours out, much to my delight, knowing that I did not want to leave the squadron.

About this time, the squadron had a most successful operation when escorting Beauforts from Leuchars. Five ships had been reported south of Bergen taking a southerly course and the Beauforts were scrambled along with the whole of our squadron, apart from myself. They were to intercept the ships at a given spot and I was detailed to fly to the point where the aircraft estimated the interception was 30 minutes later to view the damage. I arrived dead on time and made a perfect landfall. We could see a number of 109s and 110s flying in tight circles at about 500 feet; obviously they were looking for survivors in the sea. We hung around for ten minutes or so assessing the casualties until a 109 spotted us and started to give chase. Luckily I was in the middle of a turn at the time which brought me straight on a homeward direction and with full throttle we were able to hold our own at sea level until he broke off. As the weather was expected to have closed in by the time we arrived home, we were diverted to Lossiemouth. We were guided into the aerodrome by the winking of a couple of lighthouses. I had never landed at Lossie before but understood that it was surrounded on three sides by some fairly steep hills so I allowed for this on the circuit awaiting permission to land.

On landing we had to be debriefed by a 'sprog' Intelligence Officer as Lossie was a Bomber Command OTU. This debriefing lasted for a couple of hours as the officer would not release us until he had checked with Coastal Command, a delay which made me very grateful I was not involved with this lot. Hutch and I were pretty sure we had seen a ship sunk and we now discovered that the Beauforts were claiming two hits before being set upon by ME 110s. It was not until we returned to Dyce the next day that we found that as arranged, the squadron had gone in ahead of the Beauforts with their cannons and then dealt with the 110s, claiming five shot down with the loss of two Beaufighters and two Beauforts.

The next day A Flight were sent to Sumburgh and at 0300 hours the following morning I was woken and told to fly over the Norwegian coast at first light. Conditions looked fine as I went over to the Met Office. The Met Officer at Sumburgh was a brilliant character. He was a civilian and stood no more than five foot high and was totally bald. He had a way of briefing that made it seem as if he was about to step into the aircraft with you, so earnest and worried would he be. His news was not particularly good for today's flight. During the night a large front had crossed over leaving clear skies. He forecast that we would hit the tail end of this front approximately 30 miles off the Norwegian coast and cloud would be down to about 100 feet although there would be no rain.

Sure enough as we approached the Norwegian coast we could see a dirty big front to the east and the closer we got, the more it looked as if the cloud came right down to the sea. There was a very sharp edge to the front and one minute we were flying in a cloudless sky, the next we were under a thick blanket. I realised this was going to be dicey. As I flew along the coast all I could see was cliffs rising to about 100 feet on the left of me and mountains on the right. I knew it was asking the impossible when I asked Hutch if he'd been able to pinpoint. Sure enough his answer indicated that I should concentrate on my own job and let others do likewise! I could see that we were entering a fjord with the cliff faces gradually closing in on us and the tunnel becoming narrower and narrower. There was no room for me to make a turn and I was most thankful when Hutch's voice came through telling me to take the next turning to port.

We now entered another fjord. I daren't ask Hutch if he knew where we were but simply kept on the course he had indicated. The sea was calm as a millpond, so much that Hutch called on the intercom to say we were leaving quite a wash. I think this comment was a thinly-disguised query as to why we were flying so low. The answer was that I had no option. If we went higher and into the cloud I would be unable to see the sharp cliffs and rugged terrain which would be highly dangerous. At least I did not have the problem of meeting enemy aircraft; even if they decided that they could take-off they would never be able to see us. We were obviously catching the shore guns unawares as it was only first light and they would never expect us in such terrible conditions.

We turned a corner and straight ahead I saw a dozen fishing boats scattered over a 50 yard area. I had no choice but to fly straight over them and as I did so I saw the fishermen all dive for cover in the bottom of their boats. Hutch said later that once they realised it was an RAF plane, they all stood up and waved madly. As we left the boats behind we found ourselves in a wide stretch of water that seemed totally surrounded by mountains. Hutch called through to say that there should be a narrow gap in the far left-hand corner. I located the point but then had to perform a 90-degree turn through a corridor of rock, the sides of which were only about 30 to 40 yards away from the wing tips.

The far end of the corridor led into another enclosed fjord and there opposite us, hiding under the cliff overhang was a German cruiser with five destroyers surrounding it at a distance of about 200 yards. With no time to alter course I was forced to fly straight alongside the cruiser, taking a path between it and the destroyers. Catching the enemy totally unawares, not a shot was fired. We had completely outwitted the German radar, lookout posts and gun emplacements. I immediately called back to Hutch to see if he'd got every detail he needed and he replied that we'd been so close he'd even got the name, *Lützow*. He then added, quite causally, that I should pull up to 6,000 feet as straight ahead there was a 5,500 foot mountain. I went into the cloud at full throttle, literally hanging on the props but I swear I had never seen the needle of the altimeter move so slowly. I was determined to play safe and get to 7,000 feet but at just under 6,000 feet we hit the trailing edge of the front and the cloud broke. Sure enough the mountain was there, only 500 feet below us.

I then did something I had never expected to have to do and that was to give the order to send a message with the highest prefix of war. This was only to be used when an invasion fleet or a naval force were sighted. I could not help but feel an overwhelming sense of power as I told Hutch to transmit the position of the force etc. and then to shut down completely until we were well clear of the Norwegian coast. We were now at 6,000 feet in a clear sky and were a sitting target for fighters. I put Angela into a steady dive until Hutch told me that the message had been received at base when I went into a steep dive down to sea level. Hutch said that a number of stations were trying to call us but I was determined to put at least 80 miles between us and the coast before climbing to transmit again. Once I knew we were well away, I went back to a height which allowed Hutch to recommence transmitting which he did all the way back to Sumburgh. During the climb I asked Hutch if he had got any photographs. Unluckily we were only carrying the cumbersome RAF camera as there were no Leicas available when we took off and I hardly expected him to have had time to reach under his table, unstow the camera and line it up for a photo. The reply I received was typical Hutch: 'I am paid by the Air Ministry to be a navigator and wireless operator. I want more money if I am to be a photographer as well.'

The Station Commander's car followed us as we taxied to dispersal and Hutch barely had time to gather his maps together before we were bundled into the back and whisked off to the ops room. Up to then Hutch had only given the longitude and latitude position and now I asked him if he was certain he could pinpoint the position on the map. I was once again treated to a withering few sentences on his ability to do his job, but he did confirm with great excitement that he was adamant he knew the full position. The whole ops room was waiting for us. One aircrew had already been sent out as soon as our first message was received and we found another crew waiting in the ops room, all briefed, just wanting us to complete the picture. This crew were one of the A Flight gang and I knew things would not be good for them. By now all the German forces would have been alerted that the battleship *Lützow* had been found in hiding and on top of this our comrades would be flying in clear skies.

After the first few questions had been asked, I requested five minutes with Hutch simply to retrace the track we had taken and double-check our pinpoint. There was no question of it being wrong and even when two intelligence officers tried to put doubt in Hutch's mind he would not be shaken. We were both very aware that we had put our heads on the chopping block and should our pinpoint be wrong we would be in the doghouse for wasting time and effort.

Halfway through the debriefing a message from the Admiralty was passed to one of the intelligence officers saying that according to their charts, the *Lützow* could not have entered the fjord with her deep draught. I could see that Hutch's patience was giving way and he snapped back that the intelligence officer should send a message to the Admiralty to say that we had seen for ourselves it was possible and that they should get an up-to-date chart. This forceful, dour Scotsman was not to be shaken and indeed he was proved right.

Since we had arrived back by 0900 hours, there was plenty of the day left for both the Navy and RAF to deal with the *Lützow*. After an hour and a half we were allowed to go for breakfast with orders to report straight back to the controller in order to help with the briefing of further crews. As the time approached for the first aircraft to return, piloted by a Free French captain and with a Free French navigator, the wireless cabin reported that they were unable to make contact. An hour passed and the worst had to be accepted.

I knew that as soon as the front had cleared the Luftwaffe would have put an umbrella of fighters over the force. The second aircraft, the crew of which Hutch and I knew well, also failed to return and although the next two came back safely, they were unable to locate the enemy. This was followed by a squadron of Beauforts which went out later in the day, escorted by Beaus, and led to Bomber Command sending out a couple of squadrons of Halifax and Stirlings that night. Unfortunately they suffered heavy losses with no result.

It now transpired that the Admiralty had lost tabs on the *Lützow* some weeks before and that recently the Norwegian underground had given them some idea of where it might be. I was now pretty certain that we had been sent out to find that specific ship, so I was delighted that we had achieved the objective. The Navy now knew that the *Lützow* was making its way to the Baltic to join the *Scharnhorst* and *Gneisenau*. Soon after this episode Hutch and I heard through the Orderly Room that we had been recommended for the DFM once again. I could not help but think, surely this time....

14

We were now almost permanently on the readiness rota for long-range interception with a handful of recces thrown in for good measure. Somebody was definitely spinning out the end of my tour, which suited me just fine. My only frustration was that further successful interceptions still eluded me even though I was sometimes scrambling twice a day.

My luck changed one evening when I was scrambled to fly due north up the Shetland Isles and on to Sullom Voe. Directions then came to continue for 200 miles in a northerly direction at 1,500 feet. A variety of vector changes followed before the controller's voice suddenly called 'Bandit at 345 degrees'. A minute later I spotted a Blohm and Vos seaplane flying in an easterly direction. These aircraft were often used by the Luftwaffe for reconnaissance in the North Atlantic. It certainly gave me a boost to be able to tell Hutch to transmit 'Tally Ho' after all our recent fruitless endeavours. The aircraft was at about 1,000 feet and I was at 1,500 and pretty sure he hadn't seen me which gave me time to climb into the sun and plan my attack.

The sight of the black crosses on an aircraft's wings always sent a tingle down my spine. I'm sure it was all due to my schooldays when I was an avid reader of comics such as *The Modern Boy* and *The Avenger*. Wartime stories were always illustrated with Germans in long leather coats and in the background were their biplanes, sporting this sinister cross. A rear attack was out of the question as I would be flying twice as fast as my opponent and would quickly overtake him so I decided on a beam attack. I knew that the Blohm and Vos would not be able to get up to cloud base which was at 3/10 cover and that he couldn't go any faster. I remembered from an identification lecture that they only cruised at 150 miles an hour but bristled with guns. Sure enough before I could get within range the enemy's gunners opened up and I had to close fast giving frequent bursts. There seemed to be guns at every window as well as the turrets.

Seeing a panel blow off the side of the aircraft, I realised that I had hit him and quickly broke away to go below him, only pulling up when I was safely out of range. The Blohm and Vos had smoke pouring from both engines as it plunged towards the sea. Somehow the pilot kept control and managed to level out so that he was flying at sea level. The aircraft did not break up and with the adrenaline pumping furiously, I knew I must go in for the kill. There was only one turret on the front of the German aircraft so deciding that a frontal attack would involve the least risk to ourselves, I dived from about 1,000 feet giving plenty of trajectory.

On about the third long burst the starboard engine burst into flames and the aircraft rolled over on its side, hit the sea and broke up. I pulled up to 500 feet and circled while Hutch did a quick examination of Angela before reporting that he could not see any damage. Meanwhile five men had struggled free of the crashed aircraft and were now clinging to one of the floats, the fuselage and wings having been submerged. There was no sign of their dinghy. I told Hutch that I was going to climb to 3,000 feet so that he could call base and tell them to take a fix on us before transmitting in plain language that five German Luftwaffe aircrew were clinging to wreckage at this spot. I knew that by doing this I was revealing all to the German listening stations but I could not leave those men with no chance of rescue. I hoped that Air Sea Rescue at Sullom Voe would try and pick them up with a boat or Air Sea Rescue Catalina.

Before leaving I dived down over the men to check the situation, wishing immediately after, that I hadn't, as they all disappeared under water, obviously expecting to be strafed. I was well aware that war involved the loss of life but was somewhat grateful that in the RAF we were more concerned with destroying the aircraft than the pilots who flew them. I sometimes wondered how I would have reacted if I had to kill another man face to face, even in the extremes of war. Perhaps it was just as well I wasn't in the Army.

We soon covered 150 miles to make a landfall just east of Sullom Voe before flying down the Isles to Sumburgh. I was still on such a high that I broke the unwritten laws and beat up the aerodrome after my success. This was a stunt that killed Cobber Kane in France in 1939 and very nearly finished me off on this occasion. In retrospect it was a most foolish action but at the time the adrenaline was still flowing. I went straight across the airfield at 1,200 feet, judging that I could do a dive at the intersection of the runways and then straight across the crew room and the Sergeants Mess.

At my chosen point I rolled A for Angela on her back and then pulled into a vertical dive with the idea that I would gradually pull out of it. I had practiced this often enough in air tests and immediately realised as I was pulling the column back that there was something horribly wrong. With no response from the aircraft all I could picture was the poster hung in the crew room depicting PO Prune showing off and coming to a sticky end. What a bloody fool I was and what a way to go. I cannot describe my relief as Angela suddenly began to pick up and we came through the manoeuvre.

Later I was congratulated on a spectacular beat-up but not I must say by Hutch. His only comment was, 'You cut it bloody fine'. I said nothing and hoped he thought my ashen face was due to the op we'd just come back from! The ground crew's outer inspection soon located our problem, a bullet hole in the elevators. I felt quite weak when I realised how close we'd been to disaster and what a fool I was.

Once we got to the ops room, before being debriefed, I went straight to Signals and asked if they had taken a fix on us and whether Air Sea Rescue were going to the aid of the Germans. I was completely taken back when they told me there was no point because by the time a boat had been launched, the men would have perished through the cold. It was June but the temperature of the northern waters was still freezing.

That evening my victory was celebrated with pints of Sumburgh's cloudy beer but I had the worse night's sleep I ever experienced in the RAF. I just could not rid my mind of the picture of those poor men hanging on to the float. The next morning I had other things to worry about and the episode was all but forgotten. I suppose that was part of being young and being at war.

A couple of days later I was called to the phone to speak to Dave who was acting CO. He had somebody who wanted to ask me a few questions and Dave told me to speak freely. After about 25 minutes the interview came to an end and the caller asked to speak to another Sgt Pilot, Alan Welsh, who had notched up two enemy aircraft in LRI ops. They chatted for about ten minutes before ringing off. Neither myself nor my fellow pilot ever considered for a moment that we had been talking to the press.

Three weeks later commissions came through for Ossie and myself with Hutch being made a warrant officer. It was recognised that when a commission came though you were entitled to 14 days leave, supposedly so that you could be kitted out by your tailor. As it was, Dave had leave at the same time so the four of us flew an aircraft down to Dyce and then caught the Aberdeen to London train, dropping Hutch off at Dundee and myself at Peterborough. Dave went on to see his wife in Torquay and Ossie went to his wife in Croydon.

The next day Ossie and I met up in the West End having decided to splash out and have our uniforms made by Gieves the thieves in Bond Street. In the evening I joined Ossie and his wife, Molly, and we went to a show followed by a nightclub. The next evening I called into the Tivoli Bar where sure enough I met up with some of the colonials, or 'domincants' as I liked to call them, who had just left the squadron and were on their way to the Middle East. We had a hell of a night and staggering into Gieves the next morning I was delighted to find my uniform ready. I felt it was better for my health if I abandoned my plans to stay up in London and went off to King's Cross for the next train to Peterborough.

Back on the farm I worked off my London excesses with some hard hours spent hay-making. It felt good to be at home where the routine chores had been little changed by the war and so it was rather a shock to open the Saturday midday paper and read 'Potato Farmer is Nazi Killer'. The casual interview I had conducted over the phone at Sumburgh was relived in all its glory in the

91

accompanying article which was reprinted in the evening papers and some of the Sundays. My parents telephone never stopped ringing and I was highly embarrassed by the whole affair. I really did not enjoy this publicity and my only reply to all the questions was that the war was going badly and the press were desperate for good news.

The two local 'rags' called several times when they found out I was at home, wanting a personal interview which I refused. In the end I contacted Pat Winfrey, the proprietor of the papers, luckily an old family friend, and asked him to respect my privacy on leave. He agreed to have a word with the reporters although even he tried to tell me it was my duty to the public to give an interview. The only duty I felt I had was to the RAF to fly aircraft.

Amid all the telephone calls that day, I received a telegram telling me to report back to the squadron immediately. Dave rang soon after to say that he had also been recalled and was to report to Group Headquarters in Edinburgh. As there were no trains he could catch from Torquay on the Sunday, he suggested that he would be on the Monday morning train from King's Cross arriving at Peterborough at ten o'clock. He would save me a seat and we could travel up north together. I strongly suspected that Dave was wanted to set up a new squadron.

That evening I drowned some of my newspaper problems with Jimmy Lee, an old mate from the squadron who was now commissioned and stationed at Sutton Bridge on rest. We met up at the Bridge Hotel and after closing time I went back to the Officers Mess with him and a crowd. It seemed strange to be in civilian clothes in the mess and indeed the Guard Room had at first tried to stop me entering the camp. I don't really remember driving home, luck must certainly have been with me as I successfully navigated the 30 miles of fen roads, edged by steep dikes.

Monday morning found me on Peterborough Station, feeling somewhat self-conscious in my new uniform. I soon found Dave and immediately noticed he was wearing the DFC ribbon. Before I could congratulate him he said, 'Smudge, you're underdressed'. I thought there must be something wrong with my uniform but he went on to say I should be wearing the DFM ribbon. I knew nothing about this and said I would wait until it was gazetted. Dave got off at Edinburgh leaving me to go on to Aberdeen. Casual in our goodbyes, I never thought it would be three years before I saw him again.

Walking through the gate at Dyce, who should I see coming towards me but my fitter, 'Saint' Matthews. I asked him what the hell he was doing down there and he replied that he had volunteered for the Middle East. Laughingly, I asked him what I was supposed to do without a fitter. 'It doesn't matter Smudge,' he said, 'you're posted to Catfoss as an instructor.' I was sad to say goodbye to Saint who had been a great source of fun, constantly pulling my leg about my inadequate mechanical knowledge. As I continued to the ops room I pondered the news of my new posting. I had as good as finished my tour, with only two hours to go and although I would miss the squadron, I had to admit it would be great to have four months totally free from the dreaded tannoy. I had also achieved my aim of gaining the DFM and was happy that I had something to show for my tour. All in all I felt it wasn't such a bad move.

Hutch was back and I also found a new aircraft and a replacement crew waiting for a ride to Sumburgh. The replacement pilot was a Flt Lt who seemed to think that as a rookie PO I was akin to a bad smell under the nose. Although he had no ops experience he insisted on flying us which as a senior officer he was entitled to do. Our suitcases were loaded up, along with my 12-bore gun which I had brought from home to use on the squadron's clay pigeon shoot. Sumburgh was closed due to fog so we flew as far as Wick where the Flt Lt and his navigator were immediately summoned to the ops room. Approaching the Officers Mess and looking forward to a little doze, I cursed furiously as the tannoy called out for Hutch and I to report to the ops room.

I was even more annoyed when I discovered that we were on standby to do a Norwegian recce. My friend, the Flt Lt, explained that he had been detailed for it but he pleaded that he had little night flying experience with Beaus and as the job involved returning in the dark he had put us forward. Perhaps it was his unapologetic manner, or perhaps I really was looking forward to a break but just for a moment I wanted to blow my top and tell him I was posted for a rest. Swallowing down my anger, I calmly took his order and told him that I would stand-by in the Mess. As we walked out, Hutch told me I should see the controller and explain that I had finished my tour and was due at Catfoss. I just grunted. There was no way I was going to leave the squadron with a blemished record. Hutch just accepted his part as another operational trip; he still had 50 hours to do. We had never heard of a new crew arriving at the squadron and pleading insufficient night flying experience on Beaus to be able to carry out a job, especially a pre-war officer of the Flt Lt's rank. His delegation of this trip led to him receiving a hell of a bollicking on arrival on the squadron. He also found himself quickly posted to the Middle East.

It was now 1930 hours and we had another two hours until last light. Mooching around the mess, I bumped into Peter Harvey, a chap who I had trained with at Cambridge ITW and who was now flying Hudsons. He had a few beers and I sipped lemonade. The Flt Lt was sitting reading a book and shortly before ten o'clock, I noticed him leave the ante-room obviously on his way to bed. I rang the ops room soon after to see what the score was. The recce was off and we were being stood down with the Flt Lt on stand-by from first light. Having phoned Hutch to tell him, I threw the rest of my lemonade away and joined Peter in a couple of beers. The duty orderly corporal had fixed me up with a room and after about an hour I said goodbye to Peter and went to crash out.

It seemed only a few minutes later that I was roughly shaken awake by the dispatching sergeant who informed me that I was to report to the ops room immediately. It was 0430 hours and I had to be airborne by 0500 hours. He had not been told where I was sleeping and had spent over an hour looking for me. My wrath at this brutal awakening was not eased when I realised that the Flt Lt had made sure that nobody knew where he was sleeping; no wonder he'd slipped away to bed so quietly.

15

Bleary-eyed, I dressed and threw my belongings into the suitcase as it seemed we were returning to Sumburgh. The aircrew vehicle was waiting outside and we sped off to the Sergeants Mess to pick up Hutch. Ops room were in a panic as we were late being dispatched although they did manage to find me a cup of tea. I didn't think I'd better push it by asking for breakfast but felt envious of Hutch who had had time for a plate of bacon and eggs. Our suitcases and my 12-bore were thrown in and I started cockpit drill.

I felt uncomfortable in the aircraft and realised that the seat height lever was jammed so that I was unable to sit in the right position. Every pilot had his own seat setting as it was important to have a good, comfortable view, especially when flying at sea level. The fitter I called over was only a duty ground crew for visiting aircraft and his toolbox was in the watch office. When I realised that the freeing of the seat could be a half-hour job, I simply signed the 700. I could feel the controllers in the ops room breathing down my neck at further delay and just decided to go for it. If I had been on the squadron at base I would have put this aircraft down as unserviceable and taken a reserve. Everything seemed to be going wrong.

As we took off I realised that the seat was far too low for my usual position and as we dropped down to sea-level flying I tried to adapt myself to this unfamiliar angle of vision. There was no means of checking my height as the altimeter only ever flickered around the zero so whether I was flying 20 to 30 feet below my normal height at sea level I will never know. I held the aircraft at

200 feet and flew due west over the Scottish bogs and moors for a few miles before turning north and then east and dropping down over the cliffs to sea level. Hutch was quickly on the intercom, complaining that he had given me a course to fly over the aerodrome. I just said, 'It doesn't matter, nobody is going to see where we are going." He didn't answer, knowing full well that I was referring to the rumours that were rife at Wick, of spies hiding around the aerodrome. Foolish though I knew such rumours to be, that day I simply didn't want to court fate. Something was telling me to be doubly cautious to ensure that I got to Catfoss and a few months rest. I was therefore flying a few feet lower than I would normally have done.

We made a good landfall and turned south down the coast. All we saw were a few harmless fishing boats before Hutch called up to say that we had reached the end of the patrol and to give me a course for home. I remember feeling a tremendous sense of relief as I made the homeward turn. A few moments later Hutch called out that there were two 109s travelling in the opposite direction on our port side, at about 1,500 feet. I instinctively turned my head to the left and looked up. There was an enormous crash. Natural reaction made me pull back on the control column and with the speed of our travel and the flip of the wave we had hit, we shot up to 500 feet. I yelled at Hutch, 'We've clipped the sea,' to which he very calmly replied, 'I know'. The 109s had not seen us and were fast disappearing as I tried to continue on the course for base. The vibration was terrific and I could see that the prop ends were bent. We had lost speed and I was having a job to maintain height. As the vibration gave way to a complete shaking of the whole aircraft I knew that the engines were moving in their mountings. I struggled to keep level by holding the control column right over in both hands but as we dropped to 200 feet I knew we would never make it and called to Hutch to send a 'Mayday' call before preparing to ditch. This was impossible though as we were too low.

I began to run through the pilot's drill for ditching. It was important to unscrew and push aside the gun sight so as to avoid being bashed in the face by it but this was impossible for me to do as I needed both hands and all my strength to keep the control column hard over. There seemed to be a fair swell on the sea but eventually I knew I had to let the aircraft settle and I cut the engines, lifting the nose slightly. Flaps weren't used in ditching and we just seemed to float. A fair sized wave came upon us and there was a terrific bang as we clipped it and again started floating. A larger wave was following behind and just as we came into the trough proceeding it, I yanked the column back and the aircraft hit the front of the wave with its nose well up which stopped us from flipping arse over head. The engines of a Beau stuck out in front of the cockpit and we had been told that on impact with the sea it would turn turtle but somehow I managed to get the tail well down as we hit the face of the swell.

This last encounter with a wave sent me flying forward and I hit my face against the sight. All I kept thinking was that I must maintain consciousness and I struggled to collect my wits as water swirled up to my knees and blood poured down my face. An eerie silence engulfed us following the terrific noise of the last few minutes. Having pulled myself together I released the safety belts and knocked the lever on the emergency panel at my side. With great relief I saw it fall out and I quickly scrambled onto the wing and crawled to the handle which would release the dinghy, at the same time inflating my Mae West. I had a momentary panic that the dinghy would not inflate but it actually went up very quickly. By this time I could see that Hutch had jettisoned his canopy and was balancing on the edge of his cockpit. Now was the time to put into practice what he had so often done in theory.

The water was over the wings and I was able to guide the dinghy to the trailing edge of the wing and give it a good push so that it skimmed along the side of the fuselage. Hutch slithered down the side of the Beau and fell straight into it without so much as getting his feet wet. We had always anticipated that I would have to swim to catch the dinghy but we hadn't considered the rate at which it might float off. There was quite a wind and I could see it was moving at some speed as I hurriedly tried to stand up only to find that the aerial wire had snagged over my parachute pack and was dragging me down with the aircraft. I furiously beat at the release disc but nothing happened. It was only as the water got to chest height that my panicked mind cleared and I realised that I had not half turned the disc to unlock it. By now the weight of the water was holding back my arm and it took me two or three attempts before the chute fell away and I was free.

Hutch was about 40 yards away as I struck off into the water in a desperate race to catch him. When I was only ten yards from the aircraft the tail disappeared, our suitcases and my 12-bore were no more. The whole aircraft had taken less than a minute to sink. My immediate problem though was to get to the dinghy and I was hampered not only by the wind but also by my clothes. Luckily I was only wearing battledress, trousers and shoes but they were still heavy when saturated. We never wore Irvine jackets, trousers and boots when flying at sea level in case we had to ditch.

After about 20 minutes of exhausting swimming, I finally grabbed Hutch's hands and he held on to me while I got my breath back. After burning so much energy my thoughts were very much on the barley sugar that was in the survival pack but the next complication was for me to get into the dinghy. The rubber was incredibly slippery and provided no leverage for my tired body. Eventually I put both elbows over the side and Hutch stood up and literally hauled me in. I was terrified as he did this that he would fall out and we'd be in an even worse position with him being unable to swim. All I could do was lie in the bottom of the dinghy and try to regain some energy. Hutch took one look at me and said, 'What a bloody arrival'.

Within a few minutes we were able to take stock of the situation. Our biggest disappointment was on searching the pockets of the dinghy. Normally these held flares, paddles, emergency rations, water tablets, barley sugar, a baler and a pair of bellows to fit the valve. In our dinghy there were only the bellows. On arriving at the squadron, new aircraft were never allowed on an op until they had been thoroughly checked over for all essentials. We had been flying a new aircraft which hadn't even got as far as the squadron, so no checks had been carried out. On top of this, we had no escape kits. If we had been wearing flying boots, we would have tucked our escape kits into the top but as we were only in battledress and shoes, Hutch had put them in his navigation bag and they had gone down with the aircraft. As Hutch so dryly commented, 'We're really up shit creek without a paddle.' On his reckoning we were 18 to 20 miles from the coast. Feeling

98

terrible at having got us into this situation I lost all my marbles and announced that I would swim to the shore and get help for my companion. Although a good long-distance swimmer at school, I don't think I would have fared too well over this course and Hutch eventually made me see the foolishness of such a plan.

At least we had the bellows and our pocket knives. Since I was quite young I have always carried a pocket knife, in fact I would feel quite naked without it. Hutch was quite intrigued by this when he found out and eventually, after he'd witnessed several instances where it was of great use, he'd been persuaded to carry one as well. So with two knives it was no problem to hack away the canvas which held the two sides of the bellows together. We were then left with two ping-pong bats which were our paddles to get us out of this shit creek.

The sea was quite choppy with the wind in the north-west and every now and then a wave would crash over us. We set ourselves a target of 50 minutes paddling and ten minutes rest but we soon found that the ten minutes were spent baling water out with our shoes. It was far from easy to control the dinghy but our paddling was leaving a small wake behind us, indicating that we were achieving ground. Hutch drew some solace from the fact that he had a new packet of cigarettes and his lighter worked. Keeping the cigarette packet in its outer cellophane wrapper, he made a small hole to pull each cigarette through, thus keeping the remainder of the pack dry.

Nine times out of ten when a reconnaissance crew became overdue at base another aircraft would be sent out to cover the same recce. This was done to check if a sighting had been made by the first crew but at the same time the second aircraft was told to keep a look out for any sign of their colleagues. We worked out that the follow-up crew should be in the area at about 1300 hours. Letting our imagination run wild, we assumed that a Catalina would then be sent from Sullom Voe which would take a further four hours. At least we'd be back in time for a pint. Of course things might be speeded up if there were a naval force within flying distance with a Walrus aboard or at the worst, the Norwegian underground would use a fishing boat to pick us up after dark and pass us on into Sweden.

99

Sure enough at 1315 hours an aircraft appeared on the horizon which we quickly recognised by its frontal silhouette as a Beau. I immediately stood up in the dinghy, struggling to maintain my balance and began to wave my arms frantically and shout. God knows why I shouted, it just seemed to help in making myself as obvious as possible. I had no idea a Beau moved so fast at sea level. One moment he was a spot coming towards me, the next he had disappeared over the opposite horizon. He was so close that we easily read the lettering on the fuselage and knew who the crew were. The pilot was a wonderful Irishman, FO Paddy Wright and the navigator was a Scotsman and great friend of Hutch's from early training days, Pat Ross. Sitting in a bright yellow dinghy of six-feet diameter, surrounded by acres of grey sea, it seemed unbelievable that they had failed to spot us. It actually requires flares to be fired at a very specific moment to enable an airman to see such a small object below but our optimism had blocked this from our minds. As the aircrew flew out of sight we relieved the bitter disappointment by shouting the most outrageous abuse after it. Our final conclusion was that both our friends had been born with their eyes up their arses.

We continued paddling and baling and as the hours lengthened into evening our hunger and thirst were overwhelming. At eight o'clock we agreed to try and get some sleep and huddled down in the bottom of the boat, using the side as a pillow. I was really feeling the cold now through my saturated clothing. It was July but the temperature was very cool and we kept close together to share what body heat we had. It was an amazing comfort to be close to another human. Sleep was impossible however. The sea slopped over the side of the dinghy and we had to keep baling out otherwise we would have been lying in inches of water. In the end we went back to paddling where at least we were keeping the circulation going. One bonus was that being July, the night never really got dark at that latitude and we were able to just pick out the coast all the time. When we lay down to sleep we reckoned we were drifting south, parallel to the coast and that we were drawing closer.

We both reached moments of despair during that long night. Hutch's occurred when he discovered that his last three cigarettes had become waterlogged. His paddling had not been as strong as mine and we would sometimes turn in a circle, so I told him that without the excuse of a cigarette to slow him down we'd at least now have a chance of gaining the shore! In my most desolate time I suggested that we sang hymns. For some reason I'd read that shipwrecked people often did this. We found that the only hymn we both knew was 'Abide with me' and after the first two verses we decided it may be better to save our voices; anyway it was hardly cheering us up, singing a funeral hymn! Being so close to the unknown, my mind did dwell on religion and at one point I made a vow with God that if I were saved I would become a devout Christian, a bargain I have kept.

The second day found us both shaking with cold. We were wet through and looked as if we had a bad case of jaundice. The yellow dye ejected from the Mae Wests to aid the chance of being seen in the water had completely covered us and as I was to find over the next three years it was impossible to wash out. At least the salt water had helped to stop the bleeding from the gash on the side of my nose. The worst thing was our incredible thirst. Hutch began to talk about drinking the sea water and at first I persuaded him not to but by the end of the morning he quietly leant over the side of the dinghy and scooped up a cupped handful. He tried a sip, declared it was hardly salty at all and took two or three large mouthfuls. He did not try to get me to join him but declared it had quenched the extreme thirst. I resisted the temptation for a couple more hours by which time I had decided that as long as I controlled the intake .... Leaning over the side, I shaped my hands into a cup and took a good drink. The relief was indescribable and I had to agree that there did not seem a particularly high salt content. By now conversation was becoming uncomfortable. Our lips were very sore and our throats were parched. We decided it was up to us individually to control our intake of salt water.

The wind stayed in the north-west all day and we were being blown south, making only slight progress towards the coast. We would both comment at intervals that the coast definitely seemed closer but we ceased saying this as evening wore on, even though a number of seagulls had joined us and renewed our hope of nearing land. At one point as we lay resting in the bottom of the dinghy a seagull landed on the side. I nudged Hutch and gestured that I would try to catch it but before I could launch myself in the attack, the bird flew off, settling some ten yards away from the dinghy.

The weather became warmer in the early afternoon and by evening the wind was definitely moving into a westerly quarter but such little bonuses meant little to us now. That night we gave up paddling completely and just lay in the dinghy. We rarely baled out and at times six inches of water slopped around us. As waves intermittently splashed over us I became aware of a bubbling sound near my head and soon discovered an air leak around the valve where it was galvanised to the rubber. I pinched the edge of the dinghy and realised that it was not as inflated as it had been. Having cut the bellows up to make paddles I felt there was nothing we could do about this latest problem. Hutch seemed unaware of it and so I kept silent. We huddled together all night, shaking like leaves, unable to sleep. I know that I was quite prepared to give up and prayed to God that I could doze off and never wake up.

16

The sun rose and neither of us even bothered to sit up. About seven o'clock I hauled myself into a sitting position and lo and behold, we were heading into the coast. In fact there was a stretch of rock some four or five hundred yards long fairly close and on the other side we could see three or four fishing boats. We started paddling again with the aim of landing midway along the stretch of rock. Our strength was limited however and we soon realised we were still drifting, although thank God it was in the direction of land. I tried to stand up and hold open my battledress to act as a sail but I was so weak I could not brace myself against the movement of the dinghy and kept falling. It looked as if we were going to miss the rock despite our furious paddling and indeed we passed it at a distance of some 40 yards.

Hutch was quite distraught at this and started saying we hadn't a hope and that he couldn't paddle anymore. It was only when we were well past that we realised how lucky it was that we hadn't landed there. There was not a sign of life and it looked as if the rock would have been covered at high tide. What's more, we could now clearly see an island with a house on it. Distance was terribly hard to judge though. As we passed south of the fishing boats we waved and shouted. We could see each individual in the boats but they were oblivious to us even though at times they seemed to look straight in our direction. I was certain the fishing boats were within swimming distance but even I was loathe to start out, feeling as weak as I did.

As midday approached our wildest hopes seemed to be taking shape as the westerly wind continued to blow us towards the island with the house on. Spurred on by a new lease of life, I felt that we had to keep afloat at all costs. I now told Hutch that the dinghy was deflating. He looked at me and calmly said, 'Yes, I realised that yesterday but thought it best not to tell you.' In sheer desperation I put my mouth to the valve and to my absolute surprise found that it was fairly easy to blow into. We quickly took it in turns to blow ten times into the valve and after 100 puffs the dinghy was not quite as flabby. We kicked ourselves for not having mentioned it to each other before and taken action.

There followed a most anxious hour when it looked as if the wind and tide were going to take us north of the island and deposit us at the base of the perpendicular cliffs. Both the dinghy and the two of us would have been pulped to nothing had this been the case. But with much frantic paddling, four o'clock saw us no more than 200 yards from the island where there was certainly more than one house. We boosted ourselves by talk of being in Sweden by the end of the week and the UK within the month as we paddled madly for the last hundred yards.

A fairly incoherent babble of abusive relief flooded from us as we touched the rocks on the shoreline. Hutch staggered out first while I held the dinghy into the rocks and then I literally fell out onto dry land. Ten yards up the sloping rock there was vegetation and puddles of rainwater. We collapsed on our stomachs in front of the puddles, gulping the water down. It was in a fairly putrid state, but it tasted better than vintage champagne to us. Having taken our fill we sat up and took stock of our situation. From where we were we could see three houses clustered together about 200 yards away. Nobody appeared to have seen our landing and there was no sign of Germans. The landing stage in front of the houses harboured no boats.

Our first thought was to destroy the dinghy and the few personal possessions we had on us. Wallets and money were thrown into the sea. It broke my heart to do this as on my recent leave my uncle had pressed a 20 pound note into my hand. Not only was 20 pounds a lot of money in those days, it was also the first 20 pound note I had ever possessed. Although I knew it should have been handed

104

into the Intelligence Officer before take-off, I just could not bear to part with it. When I had thought of all the things I could do with my fortune, casting it into the sea had not featured!

Our Mae Wests were easily dispensed with. One rip with our pocket knives and they sank immediately they were thrown out to sea. The dinghy however proved more of a problem. I slashed it along the side nearest the rock but only this half sank, creating a fold which trapped air in the farthest side and kept it afloat. I then tried to drag it out to sea but it was too heavy and slippery for me to manoeuvre. Hutch tried to help but I warned him to keep well clear. Having got him safely to dry land the last thing I wanted was for him to fall into the sea without a Mae West. Much as I hated the thought, it was obvious that the only way to submerge the dinghy was for me to swim round to the other side and cut it. I was loathe to go into the sea again but strangely once fully submerged, my uncontrollable shaking stopped. After a few minutes I was able to dispel the remaining air and push the dinghy a couple of feet under the water. Satisfied that I could do no more I swam back to where Hutch was and scrambled out, cutting my hands on the razor sharp rocks.

Our most paramount thought now was for food and warmth. We skirted round to the back of the houses where there were small paddocks and a number of farm buildings. Keeping well away from the house with telephone wires, we entered one of the barns. There were two cows tethered and an old man squatting on a stool busy milking. He glanced up as we came in and his mouth literally dropped open. I could see from the state of Hutch that we must make a most horrific picture, soaking wet with uniforms stained bright yellow, our faces chapped and our lips swollen. After a good 30 seconds, the old man came over to us and put his fingers on my wings. I nodded and he motioned for us to stay in the barn. He then went across to one of the houses. Watching round the corner of the door, we were relieved to see he didn't go to the house with the telephone.

After a few minutes he returned, beckoning us to follow him. He steered well clear of the neighbouring houses before entering his own house where his wife and daughter were waiting. Within moments the two women produced blankets and urged us to get out of our wet clothes. Once we were well wrapped, a huge jug of milk was placed on the table with two cups. The sweetest nectar could not have compared with that milk and we downed two jugfuls.

While our clothes were put to dry, the daughter, who was about 30 years old, put something to boil on the stove. She soon served out large portions of fish which was followed up by a beautiful cream cheese. Hutch and the daughter conversed in what little German they knew and Hutch was able to make her understand that we wished to contact the underground. She said that she would get in touch with her brother who lived up the coast and he would be able to help us. She also told us that the people with the telephone were Quislings and not to be trusted. We thanked our lucky stars that we had hit the right family.

Having treated the gashes to my hands with iodine, she then left the house for an hour. We both felt incredibly sleepy but for the moment felt it prudent to stay awake. When the lady returned she spoke to Hutch. As far as he could understand she had contacted somebody and we were to go to bed for the night.

The house was one storey high and could hardly be described as a bungalow, just a couple of rooms, but two beds were made up for us in one of the bedrooms. I was pleased to see that the room commanded views out of the front, over the sea, and to the back, towards the towering cliffs of the mainland. We were literally imprisoned on the island. We also had a clear view of the landing stage which contained no boats when we went to bed. Finding our clothes almost dry, I told Hutch to tell the daughter that we wished to sleep in them, which we did.

The daughter came and sat on my bed. She wanted to know all about the war. Did we think it would be long before the Allies would land in Norway? Through the underground grapevine she had heard of the Vaagso raid of seven months previously. We tried to boost her hopes by saying that the war was going very well. Even if we had known that we were losing 200,000 tons of shipping per week, we would not have told her. We boasted that the Allies were giving hell to the Germans in the desert although in truth they had just been driven back to Alamein.

Hutch soon fell into a deep sleep but I could only doze. Both our watches seemed to have survived the wet and I constantly kept glancing at mine; the night seemed endless. In the early hours I was shaken from a light slumber by the sound of voices shouting, 'Oust! Oust!' I leapt out of bed and ran to the front window. The house seemed surrounded by German soldiers and there was a large fishing boat tied up at the landing stage. The back window showed even more soldiers.

Hutch was slowly rousing himself. Always the same in the mornings, it took him a long time to gather his senses. I told him to hurry and that we must give ourselves up so as to cause as little trouble as possible for our hosts. As he stumbled out of bed the daughter and her mother ran into the room and hugged and kissed us, unconcerned for their own safety they were apologising for the soldiers arriving. I tried to convey our thanks and praised them for their bravery, before pulling open the front door. We walked down the steps with our arms above our heads, straight towards a sergeant standing with a cocked machine-gun levelled at us.

17

We were searched and then quickly marched to the boat. I looked back but could see no sign of our rescuers and realising that a corporal and a private were staying on the island, I became most anxious for the family's safety. Sitting in the boat, I was overwhelmed with guilt as I realised that we had brought the full horrors of war to that kind family's doorstep. We had always been led to believe that all French, Danes, Dutch, Belgians and Norwegians would be only too happy to help us if we ended up in their country. Indeed, we had without thought appeared before the farmer with the arrogant, silent, request for help. Up until our arrival it is unlikely that poor family, scratching a living from fishing and 40 acres of land, would have suffered any effect of the war whatsoever. Now, because of our thoughtlessness in saving our own lives, these people would surely be punished. We were unaware of the torture the Germans and Gestapo were capable of inflicting on those who helped the Allies, but I had a horrible foreboding as the boat started off.

Obviously someone from one of the other houses had turned informer but they could hardly be blamed when the price paid for patriotism was so high. I continually tried to tell the Germans that we had forced the family to take us in and I only hope that my eagerness to exonerate them did not lead to any more trouble. What I do know is that without them we would not have survived another night.

The boat took two hours to cross the water and we were then taken to a village and put in the small police cell. As night approached we were taken onto a good-sized boat and locked in a cabin below deck which had no portholes but did have two bunks. We sailed down the coast to arrive at Bergen just before dawn, sailing at night to avoid the RAF recces. In Bergen we were taken to German barracks and given a most gentle interrogation. We told the officer we could only give our name, rank and number and he replied that he quite understood. We would be going by train to Oslo that afternoon.

We were marched through the town to the station escorted by three soldiers and a corporal heavily armed with rifles and revolvers. As a piece of propaganda this somewhat backfired as people along the way saluted us with 'V' for victory signs. The train was standing in the station but we had to wait a few minutes on the platform while the corporal went to the ticket office. Quite a few Norwegians gathered round us, trying to talk to us, which annoyed the guards who waved their rifles at them to move on. Once on the train we were pushed into a compartment and told to sit by the window. I sat right beside the window with Hutch on the other side. The guard stood in the doorway with his back to us talking to his comrades.

I immediately noticed that the window frame had a nail through the wood so that the window could not be lowered. Having settled down I gazed out, straight at two Norwegians who appeared from under the train. By their signalling and mouthing I understood that they wanted us to jump out of the window. I gestured back, indicating the nail in the frame and the impossibility of opening the window.

Suddenly all hell was let loose. The guard in the doorway had turned round and seen me gesturing to the Norwegians. His shouts brought all the German guards out onto the platform. It was like a scene from the High Chaparral with guards firing off their rifles indiscriminately and bullets ricocheting off the train. There was even a short burst of machine-gun fire. Our guard kept shouting at Hutch and myself and pulling his revolver from its holster, waved it wildly about a foot from our faces, his finger resting on the trigger. For the next 15 minutes he kept us covered, the hand holding the gun trembling like a leaf, whether through fright or rage I couldn't tell. It was an agonising 15 minutes.... Out of the corner of my eye I could see that the two Norwegians had disappeared over the railway tracks and were presumably lost in the engine sheds.

Eventually the other three guards returned and the guns were put away as the train began to pull out of the station on the long journey to Oslo. We arrived early the following morning, Friday. No chances were taken by marching us through the streets and we went by covered truck to the German headquarters in the middle of the city. It was a beautiful sunny morning and the streets seemed full of women and girls on their way to work, all looking clean and fresh and happy. I felt terribly envious of their liberty and longed to be able to walk among them.

At our destination Hutch and I were pushed into a small room which had a barred window, however there were two sprung beds which was a real touch of luxury. Our first meal arrived at lunchtime, a sparse quantity of dishes which I was to become only too familiar with over the next three years. There was a small plate of watery soup with two thin slices of sour-tasting black bread and a piece of garlic sausage. Beverages were either herb tea or acorn coffee. The coffee was just about drinkable but I simply couldn't stomach the tea and drank cold water instead.

We were again interrogated in kid-glove fashion by an intelligence officer to whom we once more gave only our name, rank and number. He tried to extract more from us by outlining the hopelessness of our situation. Did we not realise that the Allies were losing a quarter of a million tons of shipping a week? We simply sat on our beds and stared vacantly at him. Eventually he gave up his endeavours and told us we would be flown to Germany on the Monday morning.

On the Sunday the whole place was deserted and we were guarded by one 20-year-old German Army corporal armed with an automatic. He was obviously a product of the Hitler Youth Movement and kept coming into our room and, in his broken English, telling us how marvellous Hitler was and how superior the German people were. In a few months time, he told us, Germany would be the conqueror of Europe and Russia. As evening approached, our guard took us into the office opposite our room so that we could listen to the news on the wireless. After half an hour of Lord Haw Haw, he took us to the window and let us watch the the people strolling along on a beautiful summer evening. I always preferred blondes but the Norwegian girls that sunny evening were classics. Our guard was getting great satisfaction out of our obvious yearning to be free. As we crossed back to our room he pointed to the stairway about 40 yards down the corridor and shouted, "Run. No shoot." I glanced at Hutch but both of us knew that we wouldn't get ten yards down the corridor before we were gunned down. With no witnesses to dispute his tale, our guard would be well on the way to an Iron Cross, Second Class.

Back in our room, Hutch and I consoled ourselves with discussing the possibilities of hijacking the aircraft we were to travel in the next day and putting down in Sweden. We spoke in whispers, aware that the room may be bugged. Such Walter Mitty style schemes were to dominate the next few years of my life. Being a prisoner was made bearable only by the hope of escape.

By the end of the weekend we were quite confident that we would be able to follow our plans through so it was something of a shock when we boarded the Ju 52 on Monday to find ten Luftwaffe officers sitting with us. These were definitely top brass boys who Hutch deduced were on their way to the Middle East. We had a brief stop at Alborg in Denmark to pick up two more high-ranking officers before we landed at Frankfurt.

Midnight found us on Frankfurt station where Hutch was told our ways were to part. I was to join a group of a dozen RAF officer POWs who were waiting to go to Dulag Luft while Hutch was to continue with our guards to Oflag. We shook hands. I felt a great sense of sadness tinged with guilt at having got such a great friend into this mess. We exchanged hearty promises to meet in London when it was all over and then he was gone. My sadness would have been far greater had I known this was the last time I would ever see Hutch.

18

I duly joined the other 12 for our journey. None of us spoke much, I certainly didn't feel inclined to make pleasant conversation. We arrived at Dulag Luft early in the morning and were immediately searched. I made sure that my pocket knife was well concealed and was delighted that it was not found. On taking my watch the guard assured me it would be handed back when I left. Some chance, I thought, but was later surprised when the promise was kept.

We were each put in a separate cell. Being last in line I was put nearest the entrance door which in the circumstances helped to keep me sane. The room was tiny with a single window, blacked out with white paint on the outside and heavily-barred at four-inch intervals. A bare bed and a small table took up most of the floor space. The only other items in the room were a blanket, cup, soup plate and a wooden knife. My first visitor was a guard dispensing Red Cross forms. These asked for all details of our squadron, the implication being that the forms would be sent to Geneva enabling the Red Cross to inform our families of our plight. Luckily I had been to an intelligence lecture a couple of months beforehand where we had been warned about these fake forms and I simply tore mine up.

The issuing of this form was the last bit of excitement I was to know for a while as the days fell into a monotonous and mind-numbing routine. Breakfast of two thin slices of rye bread and a cup of herb tea heralded the start of each day. A few hours later watery cabbage soup would be ladled into my bowl and I would be given two potatoes the size of golf balls along with another two wafer-thin slices of bread. The evening meal was a repeat of breakfast save for the addition of a piece of ersatz margarine, the size of a small walnut. For the first three or four days the hunger pangs were unbearable but gradually as my stomach shrank so did the overwhelming desire for food.

The cell block was at hothouse temperature being one storey high with a tarred felt roof which drew all the heat from the July sun. To add to the misery the radiators were on full. The only ventilation in my cell was from an inch gap at the top of the blackened window. Most of the day I simply lay unclothed on the bed, sweat running off me, waiting for night and its slight, but welcome, reduction of temperature. Every so often I would pace the cell, estimating its measurements to the last half inch. Strangely, the figures now escape me. My one outing from the cell was when a guard came to take me to the washroom. We were allocated five minutes to wash and shave, the latter being something of a joke as we had to use a communal razor with a blade as soft as butter and ersatz soap which did not lather and smelt of carbolic.

If we wished to go to the lavatory during the day we had to turn a lever in the cell which dropped a tin flag out on the corridor. The guards were under orders not to respond immediately to such a request and would sometimes take up to two hours to do so. A number of times I had to use the cup and soup plate in the corner of the cell and judging by the rank odour which prevailed, previous inmates had done exactly the same. Not surprisingly the cell was fly-infested and I alleviated some minutes of boredom by swatting the filthy creatures. As the days went on, I took to studying their love life, convinced that the more I killed the more appeared.

My cell being next to the main corridor, I could hear when a new batch of POWs came in and I could also obtain limited vision by standing on the end of my bed and squinting through the ventilation gap. By these means I deduced after two days that some of the chaps I had arrived with were being moved to the compound and after four days I reckoned that all 12 had been moved. I began to feel worried as I recognised some lads who had come in after us also going to the compound; why wasn't I being moved?

113

After ten days of virtual solitude I felt like screaming. It was impossible to doze in the daytime due to the heat and flies and my night's rest was troubled and far from refreshing. By the 12th day my calm resolve was totally broken and when the guard appeared at lunchtime I shouted at him that I wanted to see an officer. He met my request with a vacant stare and by the time nightfall came I was convinced that I had hindered rather than helped my case.

On the 14th day an intelligence officer arrived with a chair and sat down at the table. I knew by his demeanour that I was not going to be treated kindly this time. He began firing questions at me and I quietly gave my name, rank and number as each reply. He was obviously very interested in my last reconnaissance trip; little did I know that we had been very close to the heavy water plant on that occasion. After almost an hour of receiving fruitless answers, he switched his line of questioning and told me that he knew I was involved with the Norwegian underground. Not only had I been found in a house belonging to a member but I had created a scene at Bergen station in my efforts to communicate with them. If I had not been sent to Hindoy with the underground, how did I come to be on the island? Eventually, as he repeated this question several times, I admitted that I had been washed up in a dinghy. The German's fury was uncontrollable. He shouted at me that no dinghy had been found, that I was a liar and a spy and would be handed over to the Gestapo. He stormed out of my cell and in my weakened state I felt total despair at my situation.

That night I had very little sleep and woke in the morning feeling terrible. As I lay on my bed collecting my dismal thoughts the cell door opened and to my astonishment a civilian wearing a white alpaca jacket and trousers entered. He came over and sat on the bed and opening a small file he introduced himself in perfect English as a Red Cross official. Apparently the Red Cross had been notified that I was a suspected spy about to be handed over to the Gestapo and he was here to represent me. All I needed to do was answer a few simple questions about the squadron, where it was based, the name of my CO and Flt Lt OC, to enable him to make a defence. Relief flooded through me; at last here was someone to help me out of this nightmare. I hurriedly began to answer the questions and the official wrote my answers on a clean sheet of paper he held flat on his knee. It was only when he leant back slightly that I caught sight of the underside of the paper and realised that it was one of the phoney Red Cross forms.

Anger welling inside me, I leapt to my feet and shouted, 'You Bastard'. I tried to make him turn the sheet of paper over but he kept insisting he was bona fida. As I sat seething, my jaw clamped shut, he continued to try to prise information from me, threatening that he could not be held responsible for my fate if I refused to co-operate. Eventually he rose, warning me that my foolishness could lead to dire consequences at the hands of the Gestapo. As the guard let him out of the cell I broke my silence to yell, 'Fuck off', with all the hatred and ferocity my confinement had created in me.

As the door slammed, my anger gave way to a hopeless despondency and I fell on the bed and cried like a child. For the next 24 hours my enfeebled mind ran riot and I began to doubt my judgement of the official. What if he had been from the Red Cross? What hope would I have now? To add to my mental anguish I was now tortured by the thought that I had been a traitor to my country and I imagined having to stand trial at the end of the war.

On my 17th day of confinement a different intelligence officer came to the cell. He informed me that I was a potato farmer who had joined up and flown Beaufighters. I was no longer under suspicion as a spy and was to get dressed and go over to the Dulag Luft compound. My relief was such that I did not wonder how they knew about the farming part of my background. Later I realised that they must have seen copies of the unsolicited write-up I had had in the papers three weeks previously.

The compound was about a quarter of a mile walk and I think it was mostly by willpower that I managed to control my wobbling legs enough to reach it. I was handed over to the Flt Lt Adjutant who took me to a room with only two beds in, one of which was occupied. 'Red' Lowe, my room-mate, immediately introduced himself. He was to be a constant companion and a great friend, for the remainder of the war. Holder of the DFM, Red had done a tour on Hampdens before being shot down on the One Thousand Bomber Raid. For the sake of propaganda, the powers that be had ordered all available aircraft to take part in this raid in order to reach the magic figure of a thousand. At the time Red was instructing at an Operational Training Unit but was forced to take a Wellington, with trainee crew, on the mission.

It was wonderful to be able to talk to somebody, even though we conversed in whispers, aware that the room was bugged. Red had arrived the previous day and was able to pass on what he had learnt. The main topic was food. Was there any? How much? When did we get it? I couldn't believe it when at six o'clock we went to a dining room and the army orderlies dished out a hot meal. Thank God for the Red Cross. Without their parcels we would all have starved to death within three months. Even with the parcels, quantities of food were small and I was grateful that while at Dulag I was able to lay my hands on a German pipe and some tobacco. Smoking definitely helped as an appetite suppressor.

A fortnight later we were sent to Stalg Luft III, a prison camp built in a clearing in a pine forest. The soil here was composed of about two inches of pine needle humus on top of sand. The idea being that tunnelling was virtually impossible without shoring. Red and I were put into a room with six other recent POWs, a group that was to more or less stick together for the rest of our internment. There were eight wooden huts with 20 rooms in each. Each room was a Mess and held eight officers, although this had increased to 14 by 1945. The most senior officer acted as 'gaffer'.

At the time of our arrival the camp was receiving one Red Cross parcel per person per week. Each Mess would pool its parcels and then appoint a cook quartermaster on a weekly or monthly basis. I dreaded being appointed as I had never cooked a meal in my life (a record I must shamefacedly admit to keeping to this day!). Luckily our Mess seemed full of volunteers, even though no perks went with the job.

Soon after our arrival we were told to report to the British Intelligence Officer who cross-examined all inmates in the search for German 'plants'. An old squadron member would usually vouch for your validity. I obviously reported the fact that I had been caught out under interrogation and recounted the information I had given. I secretly hoped that the officer would say something to calm my guilty conscience but he remained totally emotionless. These chaps were not trained to set minds at rest.

There was a definite hierarchy within the camp with the regulars and short service officers placing themselves above the RAFVR and the wartime volunteers. There was also a sub-division where new boys were regarded as inferior by old hands. A system of rackets and perks definitely operated and this was usually manipulated by the old 'Kriegies'. The unwritten rules were brought home to me soon after I arrived when on seeing the duty list, I recognised the name of the officer in charge of the kitchen. An old classmate from school, we had spent happy days swimming and fishing in the River Nene. Naturally when I spotted him leaning out of the cookhouse kitchen window, I immediately went over and greeted him with a cheery, 'Hello, Sam'. Far from being pleased to see me, it was only after some pressure on my part that he even admitted to knowing me. Having taken a short service commission in 1935 he was shot down in France while on Hurricanes in 1939. He was now very senior in the camp and was part of the Wings Day crowd. He obviously did not wish to know a new Kriegy pilot officer. I had the distinct impression he would have liked me to call him 'Sir' whenever our paths crossed but I did not have much time for such ego-boosting and always simply said, 'Hello, Sam'.

My chances of escape from Stalag Luft III were practically nil. Not being a miner, an engineer, a tailor or a member of any other profession useful for tunnelling, I was unlikely to be included in these schemes. On top of this I spoke no German and my schoolboy French was hardly passable. With the limited resources of foreign currency, forged passports and clothes, it was hardly likely the Escape Committee would choose to send me to the other side of the wire. I wouldn't even be able to buy a train ticket! Still, like the majority of prisoners I dreamt of escape and would rack my brains for some marvellous scheme that would astound the committee and have people queuing up to join.

If I wasn't going out, I knew I had to make the best of being in. When the Red Cross sent the camp a consignment of vegetable seeds the farmer in me took over and I claimed a bit of land outside the window of our hut. This 'garden' was to be my saviour and I spent many hours working in my six square yards. The soil was pure sand with two inches of rotted pine needles on the surface. I dug the top six inches away and then searched the compound for the odd tufts of rough grass which struggled through occasionally. If these were carefully uprooted they had a small amount of real soil clinging to the roots and I placed soil and grass on my patch of land. The idea was that the composted grass tufts would provide nutrition for the soil when dug over but the soil was so poor that more help was needed. The horse and cart that visited the camp bringing in essential rations soon became a target for us gardeners. Our Mess was within 40 yards of the entrance gate and almost without fail the horse would shit on entering the camp. I was therefore well placed to take part in the mad dash for this prime fertiliser. It was a serious business and once or twice I witnessed quite heated arguments over who had reached the prize first. For some POWs it was quite unseemly to be seen shovelling up horse manure but I noticed nobody ever refused the bits of veg we managed to grow.

During the summer growing season it was a full-time job keeping any moisture in the sandy soil and bucket after bucket of water was required. The final product was a miniature. Nothing ever grew full size in those conditions but three-inch long cucumbers and walnut-size tomatoes were better than nothing. The yields being so low, we introduced a roster to make sure that everybody sampled produce of some sort. In a desperate attempt to introduce nitrogen to the soil, I added the occasional container of my urine. Forty-five years later I told Red Lowe about this secret ingredient and he remembered me going to the latrines with a Klim tin and returning to empty the contents on my garden. He, like the others, had thought it was simply water and always enjoyed what produce there was.

19

It may have been a terrible patch of land, but my garden was a real godsend for me. The everyday boredom of camp life wore down the most cheerful of men and the constant sight of barbed-wire fences made us feel totally cut off from the world. I remember the awful feelings of absolute isolation which seem something of a paradox when you consider that I was shut up with so many other men, 850 when I arrived which increased to 5,000 by 1945. There is a big difference however between choosing to live with others and being forced into it. Generally our mess got along fairly well but everyone has habits, however small, that irritate others and these were accentuated by our unwanted close proximity to each other.

Being an even-tempered person, I suffered some small but irritating habits in silence. In my three years in captivity, I never had an argument with Red and only many years later did I tell him how his habit of shaking out his socks each night annoyed me. In the bottom bunk I would receive a thin shower of sand as each sock was ritually shaken.

I was the tin basher of the Mess, today's DIY man. I was well aware that my hammering and sawing got on several mens' nerves and whenever possible I would take my work outside. Complaints were not too numerous though as I provided cooking pots, mugs and even two armchairs, made out of the most unlikely materials. Obviously there were no proper tools in the camp and our home-made ones were confiscated if found on one of the frequent searches. I was lucky that the goons never came across my saw which was in reality my eating knife into which I had cut teeth with a borrowed, worn hacksaw blade. This blade was a much treasured possession in the camp, having been exchanged for a few squares of chocolate with a rather naive guard. Hammers were normally just a lump of wood although sometimes we would wrench off a piece of iron from the stays of the huts. The acquisition of nails was a laborious process and involved locating them in the boarding of the hut and wiggling them loose over a period of time, eventually yanking them out by brute force.

One of my more peaceful DIY projects was the construction of string hammocks. All beds started with 12 bed boards but after several requests for boards to shore up tunnels, one was liable to find one's backside resting on the floor. The situation never improved as the goons would confiscate the boards on finding a tunnel. A hammock stretched over the frame of the bed was the only way to alleviate this discomfort. To this effect, I coaxed a quantity of string from the camp orderlies who worked in the Red Cross parcel office. These orderlies were all Army personnel who had been captured at Dunkirk and they used their position in the parcel office to maximum effect, smuggling out vast amounts of the string used to tie the parcels. Having once been shown the art of hammock-making, I produced three or four for mess mates.

In all my time as a prisoner I always made a point of not discussing politics or religion, two definite hot wires to an argument. I had never had much interest in politics in civilian life being, I suppose, the archetypal, contented Conservative. I was somewhat surprised to find that of the eight in our mess, only Red shared my views. He, like myself, was fairly hazy on politics and religion so it was perhaps just as well we didn't care to discuss them! There was plenty of ardent support for Labour in the mess with three dedicated socialists. In fact George Meyer became the first Labour Mayor of Bath in 1957, although in truth he did switch parties ten years later. I was certainly not surprised by the Labour landslide in 1945, having seen the support among servicemen.

Discussion groups abounded in the camp and I found an altogether safer and more familiar outlet for myself among the Farming Group. There were only about a dozen of us who had actually farmed, it being an occupation protected from call-up, but others came along who fancied the farming life. Few of these would ever achieve their ambitions through lack of capital but it made for a more interesting group.

After almost a year at Stalag Luft III, 300 of us were moved to a camp at Schubin in Poland. I was delighted to be among those leaving, anything for a change of scenery and routine. Indeed the change of scenery was most favourable. Instead of being surrounded by dripping pine trees when we walked the boundaries of our wire cage, we looked out over Polish fields. The change of camp boosted many who had become jaded and despondent and there was a great deal of talk of escape. The huts were much nearer the fence and together with the fact that the soil was a rich clay loam, which required little shoring, tunnelling seemed to stand a good chance.

The only drawback on our arrival was the lack of Red Cross parcels. There was the equivalent of only half a parcel per prisoner and the cutback in our already meagre rations left us with little energy. We spent a lot of time simply lying on our bunks, huddled under blankets feeling very weak. When a rumour went round that the parcels were to stop altogether, the general mood was one of desperation. The nightmares I had about food were incredible. Some featured massive, steaming shepherds pies while in others I was dining elegantly at the Savoy.

It was a day of great rejoicing when the Red Cross came up trumps again and managed to send extra trucks through, bringing our ration back to one parcel per person per week. People began to emerge again and a major tunnelling project was started from the latrines. So successful was this that after four weeks the Escape Committee would not agree any other schemes until the latrine scheme had either been found or had broken out. Although a brilliant idea, this scheme was most unpopular with those not involved as it meant that half the stalls could not be used for their rightful purpose, being needed as pits for the excavated soil. At certain times of the day there would be quite a tailback waiting for a vacant cubicle.

Twice a week an old Polish farmer would come with his horse and cart, a tank attached to the cart, to bale out the sewage. He obviously had to be told what was happening in case he should wonder at the amount of soil in the sludge. I understand that not only did he never divulge the secret but that he also managed to bring in a considerable quantity of contraband, right under the nose of the guard who was detailed to escort him.

In spite of the inconvenience, everybody was delighted when the news came through that 30 men had escaped. Within ten days all but two were back and in the cooler for a fortnight's solitary. Only Lt Cdr Buckley and his German-speaking companion were never heard of and it was rumoured that they had got to Danzig.

Once the excitement had calmed somewhat, the Escape Committee looked at other proposals for tunnels. To my delight they chose the one put forward by the syndicate formed in our hut. I at last felt that I was doing something towards escape and Red and I both hoped to be included in those allowed to go. The proposal was the brainchild of a third-year Cambridge mathematics student. In the washroom there was a row of taps under which were half-glazed pipes, twenty inches wide and three feet long, set into concrete walls, three feet high. When the Germans had finished building the camp, they had foolishly left one of these pipes behind a hut. This meant that a length of pipe in the washroom could be broken away and cleared by the diggers. It was then replaced by the length from outside which simply slid into position, making the perfect trap. It was impossible to spot anything untoward when looking along the trough; certainly it was impossible to envisage anyone tunnelling there. Our luck was definitely in when we discovered that under the pipes lay only rubble and not solid concrete. Unfortunately people were again inconvenienced as this line of taps could not be used for fear of water leaking into the chamber.

Our scheme was never to be completed however. The Germans had realised that the camp was open to escape, with the huts too near the fence and the soil ideal for tunnelling. They were also aware of the sympathy and co-operation the Poles were willing to give us, so with no further ado we were locked into cattle trucks, (known as '8 horses or 42 men') and taken back to Stalag Luft III.

Somehow our Mess were reallocated our old room, so I was back with my garden. The numbers per room were increased however from eight to twelve and we were joined by two South Africans and two Rhodesians. These new chaps were a great asset to our group, being wonderfully easy to get on with. I never once heard them grumble about the size of their food portions. With food being such a valuable commodity there were obviously disagreements over its distribution and some chaps felt so strongly about their share that they would request a move to another mess. Two of our number would constantly gripe about being 'arse end', i.e. that their portions were smaller than others. I had marked up a ruler on a piece of wood to give a guide when slicing bread or meat roll and we had a marked tin for soup, porridge etc., but woe betide if the knife did not keep quite straight! I found it rather ironic that our two moaners were diehard socialists who were constantly advocating fair shares for all after the war

Gambling was a great way of relieving the boredom for many. Be it cards, two flies on a window or the speed one could walk round the camp, Bill Skinner, the camp bookmaker, would take a bet on it. Some born gamblers played for fairly high stakes and had quite a shock when they eventually arrived home and it came to the settling day. Providing the money was there, I never heard of anyone whose cheque was not honoured by the banks, even though it might have been written on a bit of cigarette packet or lavatory paper.

Not being a gambling man, I only ever had one bet which really did seem to be money for old rope. There were a number of organised sports events and in the sprint, a New Zealander and a Maori always dominated, the New Zealander always winning over 220 yards and the Maori over 100 yards. Unbeknown to most people, the Maori, an army private acting as an orderly in the camp, had actually run for his country and knew that he could beat the New Zealander; he was simply biding his time. On this particular day he decided that the time was right. Having been tipped off about his decision, I backed the non-favourite in each case, the New Zealander to win the 100 yards and the Maori to win the 220 yards. I was one of the few who showed no surprise at the results and actually made some money.

This particular sports day was the day chosen to start the Wooden Horse escape tunnel. The exact spot where the trap was to be laid was a point close to the finishing line. There was rugby practice all morning, with an emphasis on scrums, over this area. In the afternoon we all crowded around, for all intents and purposes cheering on the runners, while two men started digging. On the following day, the home-made vaulting horse made its appearance, always being sited at the same place. At first I didn't connect the tunnel with this sudden enthusiasm for vaulting, and wondered out loud at the sense of some of those novice athletes as they hurled themselves at the horse. Word soon went round that more people were needed for the gym class and realising the reason, I willingly volunteered. I soon learnt that I would never make a career out of gymnastics!

The day after the Wooden Horse broke, our hut caught the full blast of the goons' fury. We had been told to cause confusion on the morning *appel* by changing places and generally wandering around. This behaviour infuriated the guards, whose shouts led the alsations to bark and tug at their leashes. After about an hour of chaos, the Germans stormed out of the compound. Two hours later we heard more shouting and saw from our huts a platoon of storm troopers approaching the camp. They waited outside with machine-guns at the ready while the guards once more attempted to get us to line up for *appel*. When nobody responded, the storm troopers opened up with a burst of machine-gun fire and started marching into the camp. Our hut received the trail of bullets and I had never seen men move so fast to get on parade! At least we had given the three who had escaped a few more valuable hours before their disappearance was noticed.

One of the most important events in our daily life was the news bulletin. The officers and technicians who controlled the secret wireless service in prisoner of war camps deserved all the acclaim, and more, that they received at the end of the war. Everyone would be sure to be in the hut for the 'newsreader' to come and tell us the latest bulletin from London. Without this outside contact I am sure we would all have gone crazy. Like many others, I rather fancied myself as an amateur strategist and would spend hours after the bulletin thinking of the next likely steps. How the operators ever managed to conceal the wireless from the Germans I don't know. Every week, the goons would seal off a hut for an entire day and go through it with a toothcomb, yet we never missed a report. When we went to Schubin in Poland we were only two weeks before a wireless was up and running and even when towards the end of the war, we were being marched all over the place, we rarely missed a bulletin. There was massive secrecy surrounding the set and nobody mentioned it in the huts, not even by its codename. Certainly very few people knew who controlled it although I think everybody thought that Sydney Smith, a top reporter with the *Daily Express* and a lead writer after the war, was the pivotal pin.

Another high spot was receiving mail, thanks again to the Red Cross. Next of kin were allowed to send four Red Cross letters, written on special forms, per year plus one clothes parcel. My first letter arrived six months into my captivity. It was from my mother who was full of concern for my welfare and anxious that I should not fret about anything at home. My personal effects had been forwarded to her from the squadron and she had found in my writing case some snapshots of Eira Evans, my friend in Penzance, along with a couple of letters from her. Ever anxious to do the right thing, my mother told me that she had contacted Eira to tell her I was a POW and had also invited her to Thorney for a weekend. My heart sank somewhat at this news; I knew my mother meant well but I certainly wanted no ties after this war.

Eira's visit to my family apparently went very well and my mother gave her a couple of the Red Cross letter forms so that she could contact me. She wrote saying that she had joined the Wrens and was based in Portsmouth. Never a great one with the written word, I laboured over a letter telling her to have a good time and saying as kindly as possible that the last thing I wanted was a girlfriend. To her credit she replied that she quite understood but that she would like to write all the same.

I was greatly disappointed that there was no mention of my having received the DFM in my mother's letter. The lack of this honour irked me. Somehow I could have accepted my present situation if I knew I had put in a good performance beforehand. I never suspected that it had come through only days after my capture but that my parents had been told to withhold the news as it would only be giving information to German Intelligence.

When my first clothes parcel arrived, a year into my internment, I immediately looked to see if the battledress had the DFM ribbon under the pilot's brevet. It didn't and my disappointment was only

125

lifted by the fact that I now had a set of clothes that weren't dyed yellow. The visibility dye from my Mae West had certainly proved to be strong, even if it hadn't been particularly effective all that time ago when Hutch and I were bobbing around in the sea.

20

I never failed to be surprised by the number of fellow POWs I met with whom I found a mutual link with home or past life. Perhaps the most extraordinary of these was when I found that my sister, Judy, was sharing a flat in Cairo with the sister of Bob Marks, one of the chaps in my hut. Judy had joined the WAAF at the outbreak of war and was now working as a cipher officer. Bob was a great bloke who was hell-bent on staying in the RAF with a permanent commission, much to the horror of his father who wished his son to carry on the family business in Leicester. Sadly Bob was killed when testing a captured German aircraft, only a few months after war ended.

By way of one of my mother's letters, I also discovered that a Wing Commander Dick Collard had been shot down. He was married to Suzie White, a neighbouring farmer's daughter and a great friend of my cousin. I looked Dick up and spent a few hours relieving the boredom with him as we discussed people at home. On being evacuated from Stalag Luft III in January 1945, in the face of the advancing Russians, about 300 prisoners were sent to a different camp to the majority. 'Wings' Collard was the senior British officer in this group and they had a most worrying time as they were held for some weeks by the Russians after their liberation. They were held as hostages because the Russians feared there would be a war against themselves and the prisoners suffered badly. There were no Red Cross parcels and the Russian army could barely feed itself let alone extra mouths. 'Wings' Collard had no interpreters on either side and a camp full of released prisoners breathing down his neck, desperate to get home. The strain took its toll on him and he arrived home suffering from mental exhaustion from which he took several months to recover. In the fifties he left the RAF to become Conservative MP for mid-Norfolk. He died when only in his mid-fifties. At this point Stalag Luft III was well represented in parliament with Tony Barber, later Chancellor of the Exchequer and Stafford Crawley who originally stood for Labour before switching parties.

Among the 'Daddies' of the camp was a chap called Ted Chapman. Chatting to him one day I was delighted to discover that in civvy street, he had been a great friend of Ossie, the daddy of 248 squadron. Both had joined up together and when Ted was told that he was too old at 38 for aircrew, he had volunteered for air sea rescue launches. He was made Captain and was captured off the French coast when his launch was shot up and disabled while searching for a ditched crew. Along with Marcus Marsh and 'Wings' Day who were of a similar age, Ted's maturity and kindness were greatly appreciated by some of us youngsters in the camp.

Desperate to taste freedom, I eventually hit on an escape plan which I put to the Escape Committee. Everyday a horse and cart, with a single German guard as driver, come to the compound loaded with bread. Half the loaves were delivered to the cookhouse before the cart was taken outside the fence to the next compound. My idea was to make replica loaves out of cardboard from the Red Cross parcels and secure them to a frame. I could then hide under the frame and leap out when the cart was through the gates. I was well aware that the scheme was far from brilliant and I would probably get no further than Sagan railway station, but the thought of even two hours freedom filled me with exhilaration.

Tunnelling had become almost impossible at Sagan. The guards had become adept at finding the tunnels and would strike when they were over half-completed, confiscating or destroying all the precious resources we had accumulated. Eager for new ideas, the Escape Committee did not completely dismiss my scheme, even when I showed them a trial loaf I had made. The crafting of these loaves was not as easy as I had hoped. Having no proper glue I badgered the cookhouse for a few handfuls of barley, normally

128

used for making the porridge. I boiled the grain until it was a glutinous mess but quite often the cardboard just wouldn't stick and would need more than one application. Each 'loaf' then had to be darkened with a soil mixture and covered with a scattering of sawdust. For some reason all German bread was sprinkled with sawdust, so I put a thin layer of barley paste on each loaf and then added shavings. Even these shavings were time-consuming to collect as my home-made saw made very little dust. Having completed the product the only place of concealment was under my bunk. When I had laboured over five loaves, our hut was chosen for a day search. I knew there was little chance that my bread would go undetected and sure enough when I walked back into the hut, all five loaves were scattered on the floor having been well stamped on.

During the next week, as I contemplated starting my bakery up again, a big escape took place in the other compound. Total panic broke out in the *Kommandanteur* and we were called out for *appel* almost every hour. The Commandant himself came to one of these and read out an order from Berlin stating that anybody caught escaping would in future be shot immediately. At the time it was thought he was bluffing but over the next fortnight word came through that escapees had indeed been shot. When news of these Gestapo atrocities reached London, coded messages were received forbidding any further escape attempts. My great plan was truly shelved.

As the months past and the war continued, our German rations became less and less. Luckily for us, our camp received its full quota of Red Cross parcels but gradually everybody became affected by the lack of food. Energy-consuming activities such as rugger and football ceased to be played and lethargy led many men to simply lie on their beds, day after day. We could all see that the end was in sight but far from causing great excitement, it seemed most of us became withdrawn and depressed. Even friends grated on each others' nerves. Mealtimes were fraught with the possibility that someone would complain that their portion was smaller than the average. Such bickering always left an unpleasant atmosphere which would often last until night-time. For a few it all became too much and they just started walking to the wire where the guards were quick to deny them their lives.

For the truly sick or injured, there was a repatriation scheme but to become part of it one needed to be at death's door. After registering, there was a tough medical board to face before there was even the slightest chance of getting on the boat bound for home. It was quite amusing to see some Kriegies hobbling about on makeshift sticks or walking round and round looking vacant, hoping to convince the Germans of their instability.

No prisoner of war story is complete without some reference to the booze situation. Certain people were the kingpins of wine and spirit-making. The wine was prune and raisin while the spirit could only be manufactured if we had Canadian Red Cross parcels. These contained small sachets of lemonade crystals without which the spirit was undrinkable. The finished product was colourless and burnt with a warm blue flame, as with methylated spirit. The making of any alcohol was forbidden by the Germans and if the Heath Robinson stills and wineries were discovered they were immediately smashed up and their contents poured down the toilet pits.

To me, prunes and raisins were far too important a food to give up my half packet for wine. However, I did attend both a wine and a spirit party. Being shut up at night, these had to take place with people from the same hut. Nevertheless, it was quite a boost to wash and shave and put on my best uniform, even if it was an officer's tunic with a pair of army-issue khaki trousers. The wine party I attended was on my first Christmas Eve. The first few sips were terrible but then I felt the lift and could overlook the distinct taste of disinfectant. The trouble started later when both ends were trying to get rid of the stuff into the night bucket. Not one of my better Christmas Days!

The effects of the spirit party were even more devastating. I remember drinking a small cupful of the stuff and thinking that life was wonderful and everybody there was a great guy. I also remember being given a second cupful and that's my last memory for 48 hours. In retrospect I'm lucky to have survived such severe alcohol poisoning. It certainly cured me of illicit drinking. I couldn't even face a dram of schnapps offered to me on the day of liberation.

Apart from this episode and an attack of dysentery, I was fortunate not to suffer from ill-health during my incarceration. The dysentery hit me one morning and by evening I was delirious. A member of our Mess, John Reed, was a medical student in civvy street and he was allowed to work with the two medical officers in the sick bay, situated outside the compound, by giving his parole. Thank goodness John treated me as an emergency that night and managed to get a stretcher brought in to take me over to the sick bay. The room was spinning madly and my body was soaked with sweat.

After three days, during which I had eaten nothing, the doctor told me I could get up. I was so weak I just collapsed back on the bed. I could count every bone in my back and my ribs protruded alarmingly under my skin. I weighed just under eight stone. It was a great luxury to lie in a real bed, with sheets and I would happily have stayed as long as possible but for that fact that no news bulletins were received in the sick bay. As the staff and building were all paroled, no bulletins were allowed in and the lack of news almost drove me crazy. I hadn't realised just how important this outside contact was until I found myself dragging my weary body back to camp, much against the doc's orders. It felt as if I had been away for years as I caught up on the news and once again occupied my mind with the possible strategies the war could take.

My other reason for shortening my stay in the sick bay was that my tomatoes were at the peak of their harvest, (one for each Mess member, every other day). I had nurtured these plants so carefully that I was convinced nobody else could look after them and gain maximum yield. I was forced to agree to other Mess members carrying out the heavy work in my garden, such as watering, but at least I was there to supervise.

21

As the Christmas of 1944 approached we knew that the Russians were sweeping towards us and we talked hopefully of only a few more days. Some the lads managed to cut small holes in the shutters and at night could see flashes in the sky. The guards were all on edge and rumours were rife, going so far as to report Russian scout cars in Sagan. Infuriatingly the advance seemed to come to a halt about 50 miles east of the camp.

It was midday on a bitterly cold Sunday when orders came through that we were to evacuate the camp. The snow was six inches thick on the ground and it was with a mixture of horror and relief that we heard we would be marching westwards in two hours time. The Red Cross parcel orderlies brought out all the stored parcels on carts. To our delight there were roughly two and a half parcels per head. The Adjutant sent word round that there would be no guarantee of German rations on the march and we were to take the Red Cross supplies with us. By the time we had bundled our blankets and every available piece of warm clothing into kitbags or home-made holdalls there was very little room for carrying food. It seemed terrible that we were now holding more food than we could cope with.

With a sudden brainwave, I hit upon a solution to our problem and set to on my last DIY project. Our room possessed two German issue wooden chairs with curved backs. These backs would make perfect runners for a sleigh. Racing against time, I knocked the chairs apart and using copious quantities of my precious nails had a sleigh made in under the hour. This was adequate to take all the parcels for our Mess.

When darkness fell we were still waiting in our huts for the order to march. The temptation to eat some of the food packed on the sleigh was growing all the time and when a message came that we would not be leaving until the next morning, the obvious happened. We set out on a real binge, eating food as we hadn't done for years. An hour later most of us were bent double over the latrine pits vomiting up our precious rations. Nobody slept properly that night, wandering around the hut and chatting. The great hope was that the Russians would somehow arrive before the Germans had the chance to move us. We were not locked in and we could see and hear the Russian guns.

At one point we were assembled in the hut corridor and given a talk by the senior officers. They told us that there were to be no attempts at escape during the march. The Germans were likely to shoot anybody who tried. Anyhow, if we got as far as the Russian lines, the Russians would be likely to take us prisoner and they were also known to shoot first and ask questions later. Being RAF we would find civilians hostile to us so we must be sure to keep up with the main body of the march.

The next day we lined up in the compound, a most bedraggled crowd, clutching our worldly possessions. During the night a German officer had given a list of 300 names to the senior British officer. These men, to be headed by 'Wings' Collard, were to go to a different camp than the majority. I know that I for one rather wished I was on that list. A smaller contingent seemed much more manageable and Dick Collard was a very well-liked chap. It was only at the end of hostilities that I realised how lucky I had been not to be included.

Walking out through the gate I felt like shouting and dancing. It was wonderful. Not a strand of barbed wire in sight, even the air seemed cleaner. Weak though we were, we walked with almost a jaunty step as the camp receded into the background. Our sleigh worked a treat. We took it in turns to pull it in pairs, each couple pulling for an hour. I was most relieved that it held together as there were a few doubting questions asked when I was knocking it together. It was certainly needed. After only a few hours marching, some men realised that they had overloaded themselves and were forced to abandon items. As we passed through villages, adults

133

were offered cigarettes and children chocolate in an effort to persuade them to part with sleighs and toboggans.

It was ideal winter sports weather, very cold and clear. During the day we were kept warm by walking but at night the chill really set in. That first night we stopped for shelter in some farm buildings. Other places of repose were to include a bombed-out factory, a church and a variety of stables and barns. There was no hot food or brews unless we could find some wood and a match and were able to light a fire. The church we slept in lost all its kneelers and various other oddments in the name of warmth. That was probably our most cramped dwelling, with a couple of men being forced through lack of space to sleep on the altar.

The supply of bread had completely dried up and as we passed through villages we kept our eyes open for edibles. It was worth a quick look in a farm shed or outhouse in case there should be a fat chicken running around or some potatoes, eggs, kohlrabi or pig meal. The latter made excellent porridge. During the day we shared the roads with thousands of German refugees all heading west. The men were usually driving a horse and cart and they were typical German bullyboys, shouting and yelling at us to clear a path. The women were completely different, passively accepting defeat in a resigned manner. Sometimes we were able to exchange cigarettes for potatoes and other basics although bread was almost unobtainable.

The fifth night was spent in utter misery in some derelict farm buildings. A thaw had set in with continuous heavy rain and the water poured through what was left of the roof. Huddled together, sleep become impossible as the floor turned into a quagmire of mud. When morning eventually arrived the snow had turned to slush and within two hours there was not enough snow for the sleigh to run. It was now hard work to pull and worse still, the wood runners wore down fast on the hard road surface. Foolishly we continued to drag it when we should have picked it up and carried it stretcher-fashion. When we eventually realised the error in our method it was too late and my work of art disintegrated on being lifted. The crisis now was how to carry the parcels. In the end we had to give half away. Luckily in the next village the mess was able to swop a tin of corned beef for a wheelbarrow.

The thaw threw up other disadvantages. We had more or less relied on melting snow for drinking water. Now we had to queue at village taps to fill our cans. Our footwear was also highly unsuitable for such wet conditions. Most of us had only flying boots or shoes and they were not designed for wet walking. At Sagan, I had managed to obtain a pair of wooden clogs which were wonderfully warm to wear. They were not ideal for long distances however and most of the time I carried them tied together by a bit of string, around my neck.

On our sixth day of walking we were told that at the next town we would board a train and that we would also each receive a loaf of bread. The town seemed never to arrive but eventually we found ourselves in the station and there were the '8 horses or 42 men' trucks waiting on the line. We got our loaf of bread each and climbed into the trucks, the doors being shut and locked behind us.

Inside the box trucks it was chaos. There was just room for us all to sit bolt upright but lying down was a huge problem. It was impossible for 21 men to lie down along each side, so 18 did so with three at each end, their legs across the legs of the men on the sides. A bucket in the middle of the truck served as a toilet. This was totally out of reach of all but those in the centre so it had to be passed back and forth to those in need. Somehow we wiggled to our knees in front of the bucket and hoped for the best. No sooner had our truck got into some sort of order and men were ravenously munching at their bread, then I felt my guts give the first twists and turns in what I knew to be a case of Kriegy gut. Although I was starving hungry, I luckily hadn't eaten any bread as a mouthful of that sour dough would have made things even worse.

Aware of my plight, the men nearest the door hammered for the guard to open it but nobody came. The inevitable happened and I threw up the pitiful contents of my stomach. That night was spent in the uncomfortable stench of my problem, which several others had succumbed to by morning. Daybreak found us still in our siding but at last the guards unlocked the door and allowed us, five at a time, to attend to our bodily functions. For many of us it was far too late but at least we were able to empty the stinking bucket. A little later, two men from each truck were allowed to collect a bucket of tepid water from the station to make a brew. I didn't have

135

any as I knew it would go straight through me in seconds. Starvation was the only cure for this sickness. Thankfully we were allowed to keep the door open during the day with a guard standing in the opening. As dusk fell, the door was once again shut and locked and soon after we heard an engine link up with us.

Our journey was painfully slow. We were constantly shunted onto sidelines to allow troop trains through. During the day, the navigators plotted our route, peeping out between the ill-fitting boards to catch the location of towns. It was generally agreed that we were travelling in a north-westerly direction.

After three days and nights of this discomfort, we were finally offloaded into a siding and told to begin walking again. Luckily this time we had not far to go before we came to the gates of a camp. This was Marlag, the Navy and Merchant Navy Officers' POW camp, situated in the Hamburg area.

We were put into a compound formerly used by the naval officers. They in turn had been put in with the petty officers in the next door compound. Our mess quickly staked a claim to a certain amount of floor space and dumped our possessions there. Luckily most of us still had some Red Cross food as there was no sign of any rations. On arrival, I noticed a few rough Brussels sprout stalks in a bit of garden. The veg had gone but there were still leaves which I stripped and made up to a decent quantity with some grass. When it was all cooked, nobody noticed the difference, being grateful for the first green veg for a long time. My starvation diet had worked, now all I desired was to have a thorough wash. As usual, my clothes would not dry in a day and I ended up sleeping on them to finish the process.

The wireless bods worked hard to get our lifeline going but from now until we were liberated, our news bulletins were few and far between. Rumours however were abundant. Optimists said that Monty had set up headquarters a few miles down the road, while the pessimists claimed there had been a breakthrough, bigger even than in the Ardennes, and the Allied forces were being rolled back to the channel coast. Typhoon aircraft were very active in the daytime which gave us confidence that they knew of our presence. We definitely saw two race across the camp waggling their wings.

During the next ten weeks the only thought was to survive. The end seemed so close, nobody could give up now. With rations being minimal – very little German food and only a few Red Cross parcels – nobody had any energy for exercise but at least morale was generally high.

At the beginning of April we were lined up to march again. Footwear was now a big problem with most people's flying boots and shoes having virtually disintegrated. I was wearing my wooden clogs all the time which were warm in the camp but I doubted my ability to walk distances in them. The first night we spent just outside the camp. The goons really didn't seem to have much idea which way to take us and our march became something of an aimless wander. We were under strict instructions however to stay together in order to make it easier for the Allies to evacuate us when they found us. The number of guards dwindled and those left were fairly elderly, the younger ones being called up for active service. These old guards had difficulty walking the miles we covered and began to neglect many of their duties. Their morale was understandably low. They did however try their hardest to find us bread as they were afraid of what would happen to them when the Allies liberated us. They did not want any tales of hardship.

The weather was marvellous now, with warm sunny days. At night we slept out in fields, huddled together against the slight spring chill. Our only real danger was from strafing by Spits and Typhoons and as we walked we kept one eye open for cover along the side of the road. At the first sign of aircraft we all dived for shelter. The column of men stretched for some three or four miles and tragically on the second day, the tail-end of the line was hit by Allied air power, killing two and injuring a dozen. The two aircraft involved could have caused hundreds of deaths but they obviously realised who we were. It would have been difficult for the crew to see whether we were an enemy unit or not at first sight. Following this incident there was no more strafing, the crews obviously having been briefed as to our whereabouts. This didn't stop some of the lads having a run at us though, which would send us all diving for cover, swearing and joking as they departed.

We were living off the countryside as we went, plundering every chicken, egg, potato and corn store. The civilian population were now very scared and made no effort to stop us. The few cigarettes we still had proved useful for bartering for tinned foods. Eventually we came to a 3,000 acre estate, complete with a modern dairy and poultry farm, about 30 miles from Hamburg. As we slept on our first night, the German guards disappeared and we woke as free men.

The latest report of the Allies was that they were about 50 miles away, so we set about making a proper camp until we should be liberated. We used sheep hurdles, straw and timber to make shelters and as it was in abundance, we made beds of straw. What luxury after nights spent on the hard ground. Being a farmer, I was detailed to keep the mess supplied with milk. I had never milked a cow in my life, our farm being completely arable, so to save face I went off for a quiet practice on my own. After half an hour I had managed to get about half a cupful of milk in my Klim tin and had narrowly missed serious injury from the hooves of the cow. Having survived the last couple of years, the last thing I wanted was to die milking a cow so I sought out the estate workers. One of them, a Russian POW, gratefully accepted a cigarette in exchange for obtaining all the milk I needed. I nonchalantly arrived back at camp with the supply and repeated this procedure everyday for the rest of our stay. Fifty years later, at a reunion, I admitted to some of the lads from our mess that I never had milked the cows and still couldn't.

This episode was something akin to a holiday camp for us. We had ample food, no worries and beautiful weather. We all turned as brown as berries and began to put on weight. My wooden clogs had stood up well to the walk but had badly chafed the top of my left foot. The pain became unbearable one night and the next morning my foot was twice the size of the right one. I was forced to report to the sick quarters which had been set up in a stable block. The doc's examination revealed a huge abscess. He told me I must stay in the sick bay and rest it for 24 hours after which he would operate. He warned me that this would have be done without anaesthetic and the next morning gave me a rough lump of wood to grip while he cut the abscess out.

That night as I lay awake fighting the pain in my foot, I became dimly aware of a faint thudding noise in the distance. Suddenly I realised it was the sound of the Allies' guns. Several others had heard it and there was jubilation in the ward. Next morning amid the excitement, the doc presented me with something resembling a pair of crutches and told me that I would be fit to walk on them the following day.

Dozing that afternoon, I was startled awake by the sound of cheering. This could only mean one thing and grabbing the crutches, I scrambled barefoot along to where the noise was coming from. In the midst of a loud, cheering crowed I could just see a scout car bearing the insignia of the Cheshire Regiment. Emotions were running high and I don't think there was a dry eye in the whole crowd. For some it was all too much and they just sat down with their heads on their knees, sobbing.

I didn't go back to sick quarters. After all this time I certainly wanted to be on hand when my turn for evacuation came. I solved my lack of footwear by bartering with a German soldier for his jackboots. Our camp was close to a road down which a stream of German soldiers were moving, either retreating or deserting. I stood at the side of the road and held out five cigarettes while pointing at my feet. The straggly line of soldiers was a pitiful sight. The majority were either late middle-aged or Hitler Youth. The young ones were defiant to the end, often shouting and spitting at us but the older ones were totally broken. I saw one older chap exchange his Iron Cross medal for ten cigarettes.

That evening a further contingent from the Cheshire Regiment arrived and set up camp with us. The Army soon got moving and the next morning officers from the Intelligence Corps began organising us for the journey home. On the third day a convoy of lorries drove into the estate and we were on our way. That afternoon the glorious weather broke and torrential rain poured down on us as we stood in the open trucks. The Army had issued us with groundsheets which we wrapped around our shoulders and even the rain couldn't dampen our spirits. Approaching a small town, we saw Allied troops dancing and waving their arms about. They shouted that the Germans had surrendered. Our utopia was complete.

At the night's stopover camp were were met by WAAFs and nurses, complete with delousing DDT airguns. They had been told to expect the worst, instead they received a mob of bronzed, healthy-looking men who had slept under the stars and lived off the countryside for almost five weeks. All the talk there had been of what would happen when we first came in contact with girls turned out be bravado. Everyone acted the perfect gentleman and exchanged polite small talk, not even venturing into banter. What had gone wrong with us? I think we were simply shy.

That night's supper was one of my most memorable meals. We sat at tables with cloths on them and ate steak, the best meat I have ever tasted. Despite a medical officer's lecture on the effects of overeating, there was not one man missing for breakfast. Bacon and eggs for the first time in three years – absolute bliss.

That day we were moved to a flattened German aerodrome. The runways were all that remained with bomb craters filled in to make them serviceable. A few tents had been erected by a skeleton RAF staff so the majority of us took advantage of the return of the fine weather and dossed down in the open. We were told that a ferry service of Lancasters from Operational Training Units would start to take us home the next day. It was thought to be a good chance for the crews to gain some cross-country experience. This was somewhat disconcerting news as we had not expected to risk our necks with crews who were low on flying hours. For all of us, our last experience in an aircraft had been an unnerving event and I don't think anybody was really looking forward to stepping into another. There had also been an ongoing joke for some time about what a sod it would be if the aircraft carrying us to freedom came down. One or two really could not face this prospect and opted to make their own way home by land and sea.

Early the following morning we were paraded in three ranks and a sergeant counted us into batches of 28. Strangely, I was to meet up with this man 50 years later and find that he lived in the next village. I was number 28 and Red Lowe was number one, so after three years our time came to part. I was not to see him again for 45 years.

We had been told that the Lancs were scheduled to spend only ten minutes on the ground and that each group was to scramble aboard and shut the hatch as quickly as possible. The engines were not to be stopped. This system went quite smoothly until the aircraft I was allocated to caused a delay and we were told to wait. It was midday and the sun was red hot causing both Red and I to remark that the pilot should switch his engines off to avoid overheating. Fifteen minutes later we were boarding and quickly found places to sit down the sides of the fuselage. George Mayer was opposite me and as the engines opened up we braced ourselves and clung to fittings. Just as we were about to be airborne, the two port engines cut and we swung violently off the runway and went straight into a bomb crater. As I felt the initial swing I looked at George and thought, 'Even now you are not going to see Margaret.' He worshiped his wife, carrying her photographs with him everywhere and I was struck by how unfair it would be if this crash was the last of George.

Being aircrew, we reacted quickly to the problem, grabbing hold of anything to keep ourselves stable. We could have been Olympic athletes, the speed we evacuated the aircraft when it finally slid to a halt. The emergency hatch was opened within seconds and we scrambled up the ladder before dropping to the ground and running like hell to get clear of the Lanc. One engine was on fire and we didn't stop running until we were well clear of any possible explosion. The only visible injuries were bruises although we were all pretty shaken. Undeterred, most of us immediately set off for the watch tower, leaving the crew standing by the remains of their aircraft. The dispatching sergeant quickly put us at the top of the queue and we boarded the next Lancaster. I know I was pretty relieved when it was safely off the ground!

22

The great moment of stepping onto British soil was something we had all dreamt of during our years of captivity. We landed at Blackbush and I must admit I felt a mixture of emotions as I walked away from the aircraft. Everything looked exactly as it had when I had last seen good old England but I felt completely different. The last time I had left, I had been fairly carefree, expecting to be home for lunch. Now I was back, three years later, having been deprived of my liberty and having suffered a high degree of mental and physical anguish. I felt confused amid these familiar scenes.

An efficient reception committee greeted us, promising that there would be six weeks leave as soon as we were through their procedures. We were given a medical, kitted out with uniform and fed before being interviewed by a personnel officer. It was this officer who told me I had been awarded the DFM four days after I was posted missing. I was delighted by the news and only wished I had known earlier. My pleasure could not be one hundred per cent, however, until I had unburdened my guilt at having broken down under interrogation. The officer barely paused to hear my confession before dismissing it as unimportant, but somehow I still did not feel totally reassured. When the question of demob arose, I asked if there was a chance I would be sent to the Far East if I stayed on. I was told that they were not allowing ex-prisoners of war to fight against the Japanese. I therefore took my demob and departed.

Arriving at Peterborough station, I was greeted by my whole family. Bridget and Judy had got leave from the WAAF and everybody was buzzing with news. I was grateful that nobody asked me any questions; I really didn't feel up to talking about where I'd been for the past few years. On arriving home, I immediately went to my room and changed into civilian clothes. A sense of freedom filled me as the the uniform was discarded.

A family dinner party had been arranged and my mother had got hold of Scotch salmon and champagne in my honour. She was busily supervising the preparations when I asked her if she had heard from Hutch's parents and when he was expected home. I felt my heart miss a beat as her face clouded. My mother had not wished to ruin my first evening at home but asked directly, she had to tell me that Hutch was dead. He died from malnutrition three days after being liberated by the Americans.

I was totally shattered. I could see nothing but the terrible cruelty which allowed Hutch to suffer as he must have done, and which then destroyed him when he had been freed. For two hours I walked aimlessly about the farm, unable to quell my hatred for the Germans who had starved my friend to death. His state must have been pitiful if the American medical services had been unable to save him. The anger and dislike of the last years welled up in me and I despised the Germans with renewed ferocity. I knew that I must go and see Hutch's family as soon as possible and I was thankful that I had met them before and could visit as a friend.

Our family dinner that evening was a very low key affair and even the champagne failed to lift my spirits. To make matters worse, German POWs were working on the farm, living in an open camp just outside the village. It was sometime before my hatred slowly diminished and I saw them as individuals and not the enemy.

Nine months after the end of the war, four of them moved into a caravan on the farm, refusing repatriation. Within a few years three of them moved into the towns and married English girls. The fourth, Hans, a Yugoslav who had been conscripted into the German army, stayed on until his death in 1976. He was afraid to return to Yugoslavia under Tito, having backed the Germans against the Communists. Hans was a good worker who liked to be left to himself. On his death, I informed the Yugoslav Embassy but they were not interested. I knew that he had had a wife because he

143

used to send her money but I was unable to trace her whereabouts and Hans died a displaced person. He was cremated at Peterborough and his ashes scattered in the Garden of Remembrance. Only the farm foreman and myself attended his funeral and I remember thinking that even 30 years on, there were still sad souls whose lives had been totally broken by the effects of World War II.

I wrote to Hutch's parents the next morning and received an immediate reply, inviting me to Dundee the following week. Later that day, my spirits were somewhat lifted by a phone call from Dave Cartridge who was now CO of a mixed wing of Mosquitoes and Beaus based at North Coates. He told me to be at Peterborough aerodrome on Friday afternoon as he was going to fly down to pick me up for a weekend with his wing. This was a big boost for me as I was feeling at quite a loose end and felt I would really like to see the squadron again. I believe Dave had called the Air Ministry, a number of times to see when I would be back, but I don't think many POWs got invited back to their squadrons. It certainly made me feel that I was still wanted.

Standing outside the watch tower, dead on three o'clock, I saw the familiar silhouette approaching from the north and felt a thrill run down my spine. I suppose I should have stopped to think that it was burning up 300 gallons of high octane petrol just for two nights out, but I felt I deserved it. As I climbed in and closed the hatch, Dave half turned to shake my hand and I noticed he was sporting the DSO and bar and the DFC and bar. I was glad of my DFM and oak leaf.

At North Coates we went straight to the Mess for tea and I could see that Dave was as popular as ever. He started introducing me to some of the chaps, none of whom I recognised. It seemed strange to be in a Mess again, especially with so many uniforms decorated with medals. Dave quickly got that night's entertainment organised and before I knew it we were out drinking. The atmosphere was one of pure celebration. Always able to hold my own, I did not allow for three years without practice and foolishly kept up with the others until I found myself making a hasty exit to the Gents!

Much later that evening, Dave and I arrived back at the Mess where we sat in my room swopping stories about various people we had both known. I was shocked at the number of friends and acquaintances who had lost their lives. Dave told me that if I decided to stay in the RAF he could get me into his wing. I was honoured by his offer and said that I would let him know by the end of the weekend. I was still unsure as to what I wanted to do in the future, the last few years had been so unreal.

I told Dave about my lapse during my interrogation, which for some reason was still worrying me. He shrugged it off and I knew that I should do the same but I just couldn't. Soon after the end of the war the papers were full of the arrests of war criminals and traitors who had helped the Germans. I was convinced that when Allied Intelligence went through the German POW records, my revelation of the CO and Flt Cdr's names would come to light. I would then be questioned as a traitor. This worry stayed with me for about 18 months, the product of my captivity. Forty-five years later, at a POW reunion, I discovered that it was fairly common for men to be tricked by the hounding of the German interrogators. Would that I had known that all those years ago!

The next morning I was able to have a good look at a Mosquito while it was under inspection in a hangar. In 1941, I had flown down to Hatfield for some spares and seen the prototype. I had considered it a thoroughbred then and was certainly not disappointed now. I had a longing to fly one and sitting at the controls, I realised that if I took Dave's offer that's just what I would be doing. There was not much time for further reflection as the afternoon was spent on a raucous fishing trip. Armed with hand grenades we took out a boat and attempted to catch fish for the mess.

That evening, the Adjutant organised transport and hotel rooms in Skegness and a group of us really painted the town red. I entered into the spirit as much as possible but somehow it all rang a little false. I felt there had to be more to life than partying. My experience had shown me a different side to myself, a side that wanted a definite goal and the freedom to achieve it. I realised that night that the sheltered life of the RAF was not what I wanted. I wanted to be my own boss and make my way in civilian life. Perhaps I felt that for me, there were no more goals with the RAF, the ultimate one, the Second World War, had been won. From now on, the urgency was lost and partying no longer a celebration of just being alive, seemed hollow.

The next morning we went back to North Coates and I thanked Dave for his offer of a place in his wing but I told him I would have to decline. My desire to fly a Mosquito was outweighed by my decision to farm. Dave flew me back to Peterborough and we shook hands. I went to the front of the Beau and gave him a snappy salute before waving him away. I knew that my decision meant we were unlikely to meet again but I felt relief that I had actually made a commitment to myself.

It so happened that Dave and I did meet again, about four years later. I had gone down to Torquay with three friends and we were at a race meeting at Newton Abbot. Waiting in the grandstand for the start of a race, I saw Dave, standing head and shoulders above everyone else, about four rows below me. It was fantastic to see him again and we arranged to meet that evening. He came to our hotel where he was greeted enthusiastically by the barman and the manager. This did our reputation the world of good as up until then the manager had treated us with a degree of hostility, obviously expecting trouble from a boisterous bunch who spent most of the time in the bar. Dave immediately fitted in with my three friends and we began the biggest pub crawl imaginable. In every pub and club we visited, customers and staff alike greeted Dave by his christian name. His popularity in his home town had certainly not diminished.

It was a great relief that there was no racing the next day so we were able to sleep off our horrendous hangovers and that evening we were ready to start again. None of my three friends had joined up during the war, all being farmers and they found it most amusing that I continued to call Dave, 'Sir'. Amid all the leg-pulling, they took to calling him 'Sir Dave'. Perhaps it did seem strange that I could get totally legless with a good friend and refer to his rank but I did it out of respect to the man and to the King's commission. We talked shop very little but Dave did say that he thought I had done right on leaving the RAF. He found things very different after the urgency and comradeship of the war. Luckily, Dave's leave was over after that second night, I don't think any of our livers could have taken another night out!

On returning from North Coates, I had to steel myself for my trip to Dundee to visit Hutch's parents. I told them that I would get a taxi from the station to their home, not feeling that a station was the right place for us to meet. There were always joyful reunions between servicemen and their families, something I could not bear the Hutchinsons to have to witness. The seven-hour journey seemed to take forever and gave time for hundreds of thoughts to race through my mind. Was I to blame for Hutch's death? Did I let him down? Had I taken the right decision in ditching the aircraft or should I have let it break up in mid-air? Worst of all I kept thinking of him desperately waiting for liberation, as we all did, only to have his life slip away so soon after. I knew Hutch's determination and I knew he would never have given up without a fight, his condition must have been horrendous.

I also thought of the Hutchinsons receiving the news that Hutch had been liberated and ten days later, at the height of their preparations for a joyful homecoming, receiving a telegram to say he had starved to death. Could I blame his parents if they felt resentful that I was saved and their son, Richard, was dead?

My welcome into their home could not have been more sincere. Both parents seemed to realise it was just as much of an ordeal for me as it was for them. His sister was now a lovely 18-year-old who was doing war work in Dundee and she joined us that evening as we talked about her beloved brother. They were pleased to hear my remembrances of Hutch, although I sensed they did not wish to hear about the ops we had undertaken. I did manage to say that he was a fine navigator and well deserved his mention in despatches and his rank of WO. He was loved for his laid-back attitude but that certainly did not impede the way he did his job.

The next morning I told them I would catch a train back to Peterborough. They asked me to stay another night but I think we all felt this would only prolong our grief. Our parting was as courteous and warm as the whole visit had been. Mr Hutchinson had told me that the company he worked for, an American shipping firm, had offered him a post in the States and the whole family was to go. I am sure that Hutch's death had decided them on this move. I insisted on taking a taxi to the station, to save the Hutchinsons any trauma and also because I had decided to make yet another call while in Dundee. I asked the taxi driver to take me to the Repertory Theatre. Here I studied the billboards outside for the face of Hutch's girlfriend, but she was not there. Neither did her photo appear in the foyer. I was tempted to ask at the box office for her whereabouts but having no wish to cause more sadness or trouble, thought it best to leave it.

It took me a few days to get myself in gear again after my trip to Dundee but I knew I had to make another journey and do some more explaining before my affairs would be straight. This time it was to Portsmouth and Eira Evans. On hearing that I was planning a weekend on the coast, my eldest sister Rachel and her husband Dick Berry insisted on running me down there. They maintained that they wanted a weekend away and they had plenty of petrol coupons. I grudgingly accepted, aware that Rachel thought I was going to Portsmouth to get engaged. They had already met Eira on the two occasions she had been invited to Thorney by my mother. The *Daily Telegraph* was awash with engagement and marriage announcements of servicemen returned from prisoner of war camps or action overseas. I had no intention of joining the trend. I felt that I had lost six years of my life and I wanted to make up for it. Marriage was not on the agenda for many years to come.

I booked us all into the Beech Hotel at Southsea and hoped Eira would not read too much into my sister and brother-in-law accompanying us. I purposefully wore civvies in an effort to distance myself from the uniformed chap she had known before. It was great to feel the comfort of my own clothes again but it made it a nightmare getting served at the bar. The hotel was full of Navy personnel still celebrating the armistice and it was nothing for me to have to wait ten minutes to be served a drink. I got some terrible looks, especially as I was with a very attractive girl in WREN uniform. I fully expected to be handed a white feather. I only wore uniform for the few days it took to be demobbed, wanting to distance myself from my past life in the RAF. Dressing in civvies felt good but it took away all the privileges of a uniform.

On the last night, I sat with Eira in her room and explained, as kindly as I could, that our friendship would have to end. I felt an absolute shit but she took it very well. The next morning, much to Rachel's disappointment we took her back to naval quarters and

148

she and I parted with a quick handshake. I admired Eira's composure and have always hoped that she found happiness with somebody more deserving than I was.

So, I had now been at home for two weeks and had sorted out my main worries. The next minor hurdle I had to face was my official coming home party, held the following weekend. My father had saved any champagne he could get his hands on during the war for this occasion. His friendship with the wine merchant also meant there was plenty of back-up alcohol. This was to be a major party. The last thing I wanted was to face masses of people. I dreaded the whole affair but simply hadn't the heart to tell my parents. Being the first peacetime party in the district, everybody was in great form and for my parents, it was a great success. I put on a brave face throughout but would have rather been left alone in the middle of a 40-acre field.

At least I was able to immerse myself in working on the farm which provided an immediate outlet for my pent-up emotions. I sympathised with those who came back to nothing. It must have been desperately hard to dream of freedom, only to find it offered very little. Work was difficult to find and for a lot of married men, their marriages were not as they had idealised them in camp. For many others, camp had given them an opportunity to really think out their future and to mix with all kinds of men. Many came home with different aspirations to those of their wives and families.

After a few weeks my orders came through to report to Cosford for demobbing. This was carried out in order of first in first out so I was among the first hundred to be issued with bowler hats. I arrived at the Mess at midday and was having a beer with a couple of lads when I heard a laugh I definitely recognised. Johnny Woofries and I had joined up together at Uxbridge and shared a room at ITW in Cambridge. We met each other with exactly the same greeting, 'I heard you were dead!' It then materialised that we had both been in Stalag Luft III, although in separate compounds. I stayed up for a couple of days and joined Johnny for nights out. We thoroughly enjoyed ourselves although I think we were both somewhat sobered when during our talk, we realised how few of that first intake had survived.

23

I travelled home to start a completely new phase of my life. For my own peace of mind, I put the war as far from my thoughts as possible, to the extent that new friends never even realised I had been in the RAF. I certainly did not want to be a war bore and ended up going completely the opposite way, never telling anyone about my experiences. Both my parents died without knowing what I had actually been doing for those years.

I became a joint tenant on the farm with my father. The speed with which this was carried through was largely due to our landlord being the Duke of Portland. Although too old for flying duties, he had been in the RAF as a controller at Wick. Our shared background caused him to overlook the popular trend for landowners to discourage joint tenancies. I was pleased to have a definite stake in the farm but at the same time I found it hard to settle. My father was not the easiest man to work alongside and although he spoke of retiring, I knew he did not really want to. I was also finding farming slightly mundane after the RAF.

Aircrew were not considered the most reliable of men to employ after the war. Our reputation for enjoying ourselves was not one to endear us to future bosses or bankers so I was delighted when a partnership offer came out of the blue. Wilfred Treadwell, my old manager when I was at Spitalfields, contacted me to say he intended starting up a potato merchants business as soon as he was demobbed from the Navy. He would be in charge of the London site, a well-known farmer, Don Heading, would work from Norfolk and I was to market the company in Lincolnshire.

In setting up this company, I was surprised to find a feeling of resentment towards ex-servicemen displayed by those who had not fought for King and country. The bank director I visited to ask for an overdraft was a family acquaintance but this did not stop him giving me short shift. I explained that I had no collateral but was experienced in the field and was putting in £2,000 of my own money and requesting only £1,000 from him. He replied that he would not dream of giving an ex-serviceman an overdraft without concrete, realisable collateral. In the end my father put up the money and I was delighted to be able to pay him back in full, a year to the day.

Our next obstacle was to obtain a licence from the Potato Marketing Board, enabling us to purchase potatoes from farmers. Wilfred and I completed forms, giving our history from cradle days, only to be turned down. Astounded, we made an appointment to see the Head of Licencing and asked him why, given our experience, we were not able to obtain the green light. His reasoning was that we had not been trading for the past five years and were therefore not up-to-date with the market. Both Wilfred and I saw absolute red. How on earth could we be expected to be up-to-date when we had spent the past five years fighting so that people like this kept their freedom? Eventually we were able to skirt round the licencing procedure by using a licence Don Heading already held for one of his farm companies. Such rules left a bitter taste though.

Our company proved to be a succes, marred only by the death of Don in his early fifties. In 1966 I found that the farm was taking more and more time and uneager to enter the pre-pack market with all the additional work it would involve, sold my shares to Wilfred. A few years later he sold the whole company and retired.

My prisoner of war years had badly dented my self-confidence and it was two or three years before I really enjoyed meeting people again. I had a group of friends, some of whom were ex-service, but none of us ever spoke of the past. It was a matter of living for the present. I had certainly been changed by my experiences. I remember one night on the way back from a dance at Cranwell, a friend's car crashed into a telegraph pole, killing all three occupants. My war years had hardened me to the news of death and it was only when I had to attend three funerals in a week that I felt the sadness and shock that such an accident should have provoked.

My efforts with the opposite sex were somewhat hampered by this lack of self-confidence and were certainly not helped by my friends. On one of the first occasions I asked a local girl out, I foolishly told one of my bachelor crowd that I would not be joining them on that particular night. Somehow they found out that I was taking a girl to the pictures. Fifteen minutes into the film, an urgent message flashed up on the screen, 'Would Martin Smith report to the Box Office immediately.' I was most embarrassed. Should I leap up and rush out or make a quiet exit after a few minutes? In the end I took the latter course and sure enough there were three of the crowd standing grinning in the foyer. They eventually went after I had promised to join them later for a drink and I was left to make my way back to a frosty reception from my date. Little did I know that these three had already visited the other two cinemas in Peterborough with their message. Unfortunately relatives of mine were in both and telephoned me later, concerned by what they had seen.

On another occasion, I was asked out for an evening's tennis by a good friend of my sister's. Eager to prolong the evening, I invited her out for a meal afterwards. She was far more surprised than I that during our game of tennis my car should have suffered four flat tyres. By the time we had been to a garage, dinner consisted of a bag of fish and chips. Another blossoming romance the lads had managed to kill!

The final straw came when I was asked to Elizabeth's 21st birthday celebrations. A Norfolk girl, Elizabeth worked in London and as I went up there on business fairly regularly, I was able to see her with no mishap. On receiving the invite however I realised that I really knew none of her friends and would be a bit of a duck out of water. Stupidly I asked if I could bring a couple of pals to which she readily agreed. We were staying in a hotel about 12 miles from Elizabeth's home and somehow the journey to the party turned into one long pub crawl. When we arrived we found the guests gathered but everything getting off to a very slow start. We simply steamrollered in and began some antics. These were appreciated by some but not by all, least of all Elizabeth's father whom Nic Vergette mistook for a waiter serving drinks. As we left at the end of the evening, our hostess asked us to return the next day for lunchtime drinks. Our morning-after courage was far from strong however and with the distinct feeling we may have been slightly too lively, I rang to make a weak excuse for our absence. Goodbye to that promising start!

The thrill I had always got from flying had to be replaced by something and I eventually found the answer in hunting and point-to-pointing. Always an avid National Hunt spectator I simply took it one further and bought a horse. For me point-to-pointing was in many ways on a par with ops. On the morning of the race I would experience the first stomach butterflies, similar to the ops briefing. Then came the saddling up which compared to cockpit drill. As soon as I was on the horse's back and cantering down to the start my butterflies would disappear, exactly as when taxiing for take-off. The race over, I would walk back to the unsaddling enclosure on a terrific high just as when taxiing back to dispersal. Even the wind down at night followed the same pattern, usually going out to a party and not returning till the early hours of the following morning. I didn't take up point-to-point riding until I was 28, an age at which some people contemplate retiring from the sport, but I managed to continue until I was 42.

I had some pretty hairy experiences point-to-pointing but always thrived on the thrill. I remember one of my first races when two fences out there were only the favourite and myself still standing. I knew I had him beaten as I hadn't moved on my horse and he was struggling to keep upside with me. But the other jockey was very experienced and an old hand at the job and he knew I was riding a novice. He very cleverly shouted at his horse making my animal take off too soon and crash through the fence. It was just a question of baling out. When I picked myself up the horse was heading for the next parish. Luckily some two or three fields away a chap caught him and obviously fancying himself as a jockey jumped on his back and with legs and arms waving in the air, galloped back to where I was. He legged me up and I jumped the last two fences to get second place and the fifteen quid that went with it.

When I went into the weighing room, Jack was there with a grin on his face. One sometimes has to learn the hard way from the veterans. The secretary told me I would be disqualified as I had taken too long but he admitted that nobody had taken the time behind the winner. I jokingly said that if the fifteen quid was not in the post on Monday he would be sorry. The cheque was duly received.

On another occasion, I was five lengths in front at the last fence, riding a horse I had never raced before. I was certain nothing could beat me. Unfortunately, the run-in to the winning post was lined with four-foot chestnut paling. When my horse landed over the last fence all he could see was this paling. He took hold and went straight for it and I was simply a passenger. So 50 yards from the post we sailed over the fencing straight onto the Duke of Gloucester's gleaming, deep-mauve Rolls Royce. We scratched the front wing with a hoof but cleverly managed to land in the five-foot square gap between the fence and the Rolls radiator. I think the horse was so surprised to find himself where he was that after dodging a few more cars I was able to pull him up.

It was through point-to-pointing that I met John Waterworth. John would often come out with our crowd and would sometimes bring his younger sister Margaret. Margaret never seemed short of people to take her out but eventually I plucked up courage and asked her out to dinner. Two days before, I was struck down with mumps and feeling a real idiot, rang to cancel. I did however arrange to take her to a dance. It was a brilliant evening until things got slightly too boisterous. Two or three of us jumped onto a beam above the dance floor and proceeded to do a 'hand over hand' along it. Almost at the far end, I lost my balance and fell with a thud on my knee. I knew something was wrong and could only sit in agony as Margaret, John and his wife Joy drove me the 30 miles to Peterborough hospital.

The next morning my kneecap was removed. I had visions of spending the rest of my life lame, only able to walk with the aid of a stick and at first I pleaded with the surgeon to try to mend it. He insisted that in time the muscle would function as a kneecap and indeed he was quite right. I have never had any problem with that knee at all. Within three months I was walking normally and able to ride. Once mobile, I called Margaret and was most relieved when she agreed to attempt a third date. This time things went according to plan and within a few months I proposed.

24

We finally married on a snowy January day in 1956. Our reception was at Peterborough town hall and was a wonderful party which we were quite loathe to leave in order to catch the London train for a honeymoon in Switzerland. After a riotous send-off to the station, we found that our train was delayed and so settled ourselves in the refreshment room for a quiet drink. Word somehow got back to the town hall concerning the delay and before we knew it our guests came to the station to carry on the party. When eventually our train arrived, we were bundled into a crowded compartment along with handfuls of confetti, much to the amusement of the other passengers.

They say farming is a way of life and it is certainly one which I enjoyed right up until my mid-sixties. Having two daughters and no son to pass the farm on to, I was advised at this stage to retire. At first I was aghast at such a suggestion, surely all farmers go on until they drop? Over the course of the following year, however, I began to realise the speed at which farming was changing. With no young imput I found the techniques of modern farming were beyond me. Burying my pride, I acknowledged that my time was up and within a matter of months I was an ex-farmer. The shock of retirement was overwhelming. Suddenly it seemed as if I had no purpose to my life.

Within a couple of weeks I was having a glass of sherry at midday. This was totally uncharacteristic as I never drank in the day and hardly touched anything but beer. I just felt in desperate need of something to get me through the seemingly empty days.

Unfortunately it was not long before alcohol became my complete solace and I would drink a couple of bottles of sherry each day. Displaying the typical attributes of an alcoholic I was anti-social and unreasonable, although never violent. I was engulfed in self-pity and oblivious to the distress I caused Margaret and my daughters.

For Margaret, this period must have been hell but she shouldered all the added responsibility my drinking gave her and ensured that our life went on. Eventually she persuaded me to go to see our family doctor, Dr. Tweedie and with the help of my sister, Rachel, who took on the thankless task of taking me to the appointment, I was made to go.

Dr Tweedie was most helpful, but the only solution he could offer was that I went to a private clinic to dry out. As he explained, there were few national health facilities. In my depressed state, I was convinced that I was broke and would not entertain the idea of paying for any help, especially for something I had brought on myself. Instead I offered to go to Alcoholics Anonymous which I did, in spite of Dr Tweedie's lack of conviction about the help I would obtain. Indeed two sessions listening to lectures by sanctimonious ex-alcoholics was enough for me. I couldn't get home fast enough to get a drink.

A few weeks later, Dr Tweedie asked me to go and see him again and he told me there was a place in a national health clinic in Peterborough, run by Dr Vaysey. I was to be there that day. Of course I pleaded every excuse under the sun as to why I couldn't go but the combined desperation of Margaret and Rachel forced me into the car and saw me installed in the clinic that night.

I was put into a small room with bars at the window and forced to take some tablets which knocked me out. I woke with horror to the realisation that I was once more a prisoner. This time though it was definitely my own fault. Not only could I see bars at the window but there was also a high chain-link fence surrounding the house. To my mind the male and female nurses were nothing short of guards albeit without rifles and revolvers. By coincidence I had visited this same house as a child for birthday parties and was vaguely familiar with the layout. What I was not familiar with was the type of patients who were now its occupants. These were

Peterborough's real down-and-out drug and drink addicts. Full of self-pity I rang Rachel and begged her to take me away from this place. Rachel weakened but I then made the mistake of ringing Margaret. My sob story cut no ice with her; she was only too aware that this was my only chance. Painful though it must have been for her she forbade Rachel to come and take me home.

After two nights in the single room I was moved into the dormitory of 12 beds. Far from the comradeship I drew comfort from when in the POW mess, I felt total isolation here. The nights were broken by the moans of addicts and quite often the police would come in, bringing another man found on the streets. At my first meeting with Dr Vaysey I told him that the clinic could not possibly help me and that I must be allowed to leave. He quietly told me that I was quite free to go at any time but that having done so I would never be readmitted. His whole manner touched something inside me and I felt some small hope that I could be cured. The treatment, I was told would take at least three weeks.

Back in the dormitory I weighed up what Dr Vaysey had said. I was relieved to know how long I was to be there. Three weeks was nothing when I compared it with three years of captivity. At least I knew the length of my sentence this time. I decided to stay and can only express my infinite gratitude to Dr Vaysey and his team for the work they put into me. When 'liberation day' came I found my desire for alcohol had gone.

My cure was put to the test a few days later when I travelled up to Scotland by train to stay with my sister, Judy. I knew the five-hour journey would be tedious and I made a point of sitting near the buffet bar. Almost immediately I got into conversation with the chap opposite and never once felt the need for a drink. The Scottish air proved invigorating enough without alcohol which was just as well as Judy had made sure there was not a drop to be seen. I had to laugh on my last evening when I insisted I treat her to a meal out. We went to a local hotel and on arriving I told her to go through to the lounge while I ordered our drinks from the bar. The barman had only just opened up and asked me if I'd mind waiting a minute while he fetched some bottles. This took some ten minutes and when I finally took our drinks through to the lounge, Judy was in a real state, convinced that I had been having a major session in the bar. Within a month of being home I found that I could drink sociably with no desire to go any further. I also discovered that few people had even realised my problem, such is the deviousness of the alcoholic. I was therefore very lucky in being able to pick up my life where I had left off, 15 months earlier. I am most fortunate to have a wife who stood by me and enabled this to happen.

Some months later I was at an RAF POW reunion and the topic of alcohol came up. There were five of us present and all revealed that at one time or another we had taken to the bottle. Those years of captivity certainly had something to answer for.

It was only after my retirement and the period of drinking that I began to feel an interest in what had happened during the war years. Out of the blue I received a phone call from Red Lowe, my companion from when I first shared a room at Dulag Luft to when we shook hands and boarded separate aircraft back to Britain. After 45 years he had set out to trace me, helped by British Telecom. I also discovered that Hank Staniland, a great friend at Stalag Luft, had retired to a village nearby. I arranged for the three of us and our wives to meet up for an evening at my local pub. I was to stand the meal.

Our landlord, Rick Podmore was something of an RAF buff and when I told him I wished to put on a POW meal he came up trumps. I told Red and Hank that I had ordered the set dinner. The six of us sat through a first course of watery soup with a cabbage leaf floating on each bowl. This was followed by a very thin slice of bully beef, a small piece of sour black bread and a couple of unpeeled potatoes. It was only when the desert of barley porridge was served from a bucket that the penny clicked. They had all been suffering in silence, thinking what a ghastly meal it was but not liking to complain as I was footing the bill. We cleared the plates and sat down to a fantastic meal.

After that enjoyable night we had a number of reunions at the pub. Word got round and we soon found that our numbers swelled with ex-RAF and Second World War buffs. Red Lowe had kept in contact with other members of our mess. Five of them had died in their mid-fifties and the sixth, Georgie Meyer was in very poor health. However, as he did not live far from Red, they came up together for a night. Georgie was in great form but was obviously ill and he died shortly afterwards in August 1993. While a POW Georgie had borne the additional burden of being a Jew. He had to be extra vigilant and keep a very low profile with the Germans.

It was only when we began these reunions that I at last let myself relive my wartime experiences. Since liberation day I had kept everything bottled inside me. I never did tell my parents what I had been through and even Margaret only discovered I had been in the RAF and a prisoner of war some 18 months after we met. Indeed, I did not bother to claim my campaign medals until a couple of years ago, 45 years after they were earned. I was eager to put those years behind me but perhaps I did too thorough a job. Perhaps I would have saved myself my alcoholic bout had I felt able to open up beforehand. The very idea of writing a book would have been totally abhorrent a few years ago. Indeed it was only with the encouragement of Peter Crew, a friend who some years before had read my logbook, that I decided to have a go. If nothing else, at least it is a tale of survival.

25

APRIL 1995

My story should be finished. I have done what I set out to do and my experiences are all recorded. So why do I still have a feeling of unfinished business?

It was only when the final chapters were written that I realised these memories would not be complete unless I went to Norway, visited the island Hutch and I drifted to and, hopefully, met any survivors of the family who undoubtedly saved our lives. Having suppressed all thoughts of our capture for so many years, I now found it was imperative for my peace of mind that I returned to Norway.

My initial plan was to go for a long weekend, hire a fishing boat and hope to recognise the island, based on the memory of my final reconnaissance. I was somewhat floored when I realised that the reconnaissance covered a 60-mile stretch of coastline with hundreds of islands scattered along it. Obviously I was going to have to be a little more methodical in my approach, so I began by recalling everything I could about the island's position.

Luckily, I had listened to Hutch's briefing before that final flight. Usually I would go and have a chat with the met officer while Hutch was briefed but that day I didn't and I could still remember the pinpoint at the end of the recce. Combined with this, I have never forgotten the figure 232 degrees which is the last course Hutch ever gave me. The reciprocal of this gave me a position on the Norwegian coast, although I then had to deduce whether Hutch's course for home was aimed at Sumburgh or the middle of the Shetland Isles. Bearing in mind that the weather and visibility had been good, I decided that we would have been aiming for Sumburgh.

The actual outline of the island as we drifted towards it has always remained a clear picture and I could also recall the wind directions. We drifted south-south-easterly in the north-north-westerly wind for approximately 45 hours, followed by an easterly drift for some 15 hours when we were caught in a light to moderate westerly wind.

When we left the island, in the company of our German guards, we travelled by boat for two hours in a north-easterly direction at about four to five miles an hour. We were unable to see the name of the village we arrived at, but I remember that it was fairly large. Our next journey was undertaken in the hold of a small coastal boat. Although unable to see out, we both reckoned we were travelling in a southerly direction. After six hours at a speed I estimated to be about eight to nine miles per hour there was no disputing our destination as Bergen.

So, there were all my facts. Now I had to pinpoint the island. I managed to procure some very good maps and spent several evenings armed with a protractor, compass and glass of wine, (essential for stimulating the memory after 53 years) searching through the maze of dots and blobs which pass for islands. At last I decided that the island was Malvaer and that the village the Germans had taken us to was Florelandet.

Eager to have my calculations verified, Peter Crew contacted the Norwegian Embassy to see if they could do this. Two months later they came back to say there was no record of anyone being taken prisoner on Malvaer, however they put us in touch with the Mayoress of Askvoll, Kjellaug Hoyvik, whose kommune covered this area. Again months passed before we heard that they were unable to find any information. The underground had kept no documents or diaries of their activities and the Quisling government had destroyed most of their papers in the closing stages of the war. However, Kjellaug Hoyvik told us she would put something in the local press to see if any memories could be jogged.

As time elapsed, I began to think we were trying the impossible, that we couldn't possibly find a small Norwegian island on the basis of recollections from 50 years ago. On the other hand, the island had to still exist, and every aspect of its terrain, three houses and a cattle shed were vivid in my mind.

Then out of the blue I received a letter from a Norwegian called Jorgen Stang who lived in Strongfjorden. He had just returned to Norway after a period overseas and had heard of our enquiries. He wrote to say that as a small boy in the summer of 1942, he watched two RAF aircrew being escorted from the German garrison to the quay of Strongfjorden. He remembered them giving victory signs to the local people. This mention of our defiant gesture convinced me that at last we had a lead. It was Strongfjorden, not Florelandet, that we were first taken to.

My delight at this breakthrough was short-lived however. Further enquiries led to a frustrating silence. In fact I doubt we would have got any further at all had it not been for the intervention of Group Captain Christopher Granville-White C.B.E., (Hoppy). A near neighbour, he became interested in our search and asked if he could be of assistance. At the time he was working at the Ministry of Defence and he felt he might be able to build on the scant information we had. Indeed, a fortnight later he told me he had met a Norwegian Air Force General at a Norwegian Embassy reception and had talked to him about our project.

The next day the general and Hoppy had contacted a Norwegian officer, Colonel Sandnes, working in a command headquarters in Stavanger who was interested in the history of the war years and had access to all archives. A great deal of correspondence now went on between Hoppy, Colonel Sandnes and the Mayoress and Kommune administrator, Paal Fennell. Everything pointed to the island being that of Hindoy.

I really wanted to believe this was the island we'd been searching for, but I was worried by the detail on my maps. Only two houses were shown on Hindoy and I knew there had been three on the island we'd landed on. Once again Hoppy came to my rescue. A friend of his, Wing Commander Harper of 41 Squadron was taking a flight of Jaguars to Norway for a month's combined exercise. He kindly agreed to help me with my research while in Norway.

The resulting data was all I needed to convince me that yes, we had found the right island. Wing Commander Harper managed to procure some photos of the island and not only did they show three houses, but right in the middle of the island was the wooden cowshed where Hutch and I first made contact with the farmer. I was amazed to see it still standing after 53 years – it was not in the best of repair in 1942!

I was now only too happy to accept the invitation I had received from the Askvoll Kommune to share their VE Day celebrations with them. In need of moral support, I contacted Red Lowe, my running mate of POW days and was delighted when he agreed to make the trip with me. As Hoppy continued to liaise with Askvoll about our arrangements, I began to realise however that this was a far bigger venture than two old codgers like Red and I could cope with. We needed the masterminds of the whole operation with us and I lost no time in asking Peter Crew and Hoppy if they would come to Norway. Reluctant at first to infringe on what they viewed as our celebrations, I painted a pitiful picture of Red and I as two old-age pensioners alone in Norway. I don't know if they really swallowed the story, but they agreed to come! The Ministry of Defence made the visit official so Hoppy was promoted to be our senior British officer and Peter became our civilian Adjutant. By the end of March, with the trip only five weeks away, my main concern was that there was still no trace of the family who had taken Hutch and myself in. I was worried about the reprisals that may have been carried out by the Germans and although I looked forward to going to Hindoy I did not feel I could enjoy the Askvoll celebrations if the family had suffered on my behalf. I was delighted therefore to receive a letter from the Kommune in early April giving details of the families who lived on the island in 1942.

The old people who had taken us in were dead but their daughter, Hjordis Johanne Spord, (Skalde), was still alive and living near Bergen. At 88, Hjordis was not in good health but both she and her son wanted to see me. Jenny Marie Vaeroy, (Heggoy), was the surviving daughter of the other family living on Hindoy. Apparently as an 18-year-old, she had watched us land our dinghy and had followed us at a safe distance as we made our way onto the island. Jenny's family were heavily involved with the underground, but her brothers were out fishing when she saw us and she naturally did not want to approach us on her own. She had however asked to meet me on this return visit to Norway. Unfortunately, due to a family bereavement the meeting with Jenny never took place.

So, Friday 5 May 1995 saw Hoppy, Peter, Red and myself at Heathrow waiting for our flight to Bergen. Everything seemed to be going to plan until we'd passed through passport control. Like a fool, I'd left my glasses on a table in the departure lounge. Peter and I tried unsuccessfully to go back, much to Hoppy's amusement. He felt that, as a former POW, I would realize that once processed and inside, it would be impossible to go back. The British officials were unbending and the former POW was trapped again!

We spent the night in Bergen and on Saturday morning made our way to Bergen station. Vivid memories were unfurled as I found myself walking through the same entrance that I had been marched through in July 1942. Apart from a modern ticket office, Bergen station is unchanged since the war and I found myself standing in the exact entrance hall where I stood with my German guards. I then went out on to the platform where I had sat on the train and watched hopefully as the partisans tried to effect my escape. It seemed impossible that 53 years had passed.

It was now time to board the boat to Askvoll. Two and a half hours later we were being greeted by Alfred Vorland, Head of Office of the Askvoll Kommune Administration on the quay of the tiny habitation. We spent a pleasant evening looking round the area but I was already beginning to feel nervous about our visit to Hindoy the next day. What if Hindoy wasn't the island?

As Hoppy gave us our daily briefing at breakfast the next morning I just had to voice my fears. These were met with a deadly hush, and then some fast planning. Whatever happened I was to pretend Hindoy was the island. Even if I didn't recognise it from Adam, I was to carry on as if this were where we landed all those years ago. So much effort had been made on the part of the people of Askvoll that we couldn't disappoint them.

We now met the Mayoress of Askvoll, Kjellaug Hoyvik, who was to accompany us on the trip. She was a wonderful lady who soon captured our hearts with her charm and openness. As the party assembled to wait for the Mayoress's boat, I became more and more nervous. Luckily I managed to buy a packet of cigarettes and, although I had given up smoking some years before, began to steadily chain-smoke my way through them.

We boarded the boat with everyone, excluding myself, in high spirits. Hoppy had brought along an RAF ensign and this was raised to fly alongside the boat's Norwegian flag. Within 15 minutes the island of Hindoy came into view. All my fears were confirmed. No way was this my island. Forgetting our careful plans at breakfast, I could not help but voice my disappointment. An immediate silence fell over everybody. Hoppy now suggested that the island was unrecognisable because of the angle we were approaching from. He asked the captain to head back out to sea and approach from a westerly direction. As the boat changed course, I felt the disappointment of the whole group and wished I could just jump overboard and set course for the Shetlands!

We sped out to sea for about three miles until we came abreast of a small rocky outcrop, (Moldvaer). My heart leapt as I spotted a tiny wooden shed perched on the rocks. At midday all those years ago, I had passed this exact spot. Indeed this was where Hutch and I had first tried to land. I simply couldn't believe how time had stood still. We now turned onto an easterly course and there, a few miles ahead was what I had come to Norway to find.

I remembered the agonising five hours it had taken Hutch and I to travel between Moldvaer and Hindoy as today our boat covered the distance in a matter of minutes. I was now able to direct the boat to the exact spot where we had finally clambered out of the dinghy onto dry land. We went within ten yards of the shore and the small sloping cliff up which we had scrambled, before heading round to the east side of the island. There was the same improvised landing stage that I had been marched onto under guard. I lost no time in climbing out, a free man.

I immediately set off across the little island to the point where we had finally destroyed the dinghy. Words simply failed me, and still do. I felt that I had always been there. For 53 years I had lived with the constant memory of this place and now it was a reality again. Even the two crevices in the rock, where we had taken our first drink of fresh water, were unaltered. I lay down flat on the my stomach and once again drank from them. The taste was the same, a brackish, salty tang, but I remembered it as nectar after salt water.

An absolute non-believer in spiritualism, I find it hard to admit that as I lay at that puddle, I felt Hutch at my side. For a few seconds his presence was as definite as the ground I lay on and it was with a feeling of great relief that I stood up and saw my current companions. For the whole duration of our visit to the island I felt a strange awareness and affinity to the past, which for a man as practical as myself came as something of a shock.

From the cliff I retraced our steps to the cowshed where we had made contact with the farmer and then walked across to the house. This was in good order and still used by the Spord family as a holiday home. Standing outside, I suddenly felt that everyone was taking the trip a little too seriously, partly I should imagine because of my own obvious emotion. So I raised my hands above my head and walked, as before in surrender, down the steps of the house to the landing stage.

When the time came to board the boat back to Askvoll, I did so feeling quite exhausted but at the same time strangely peaceful. A pschycologist would probably have a field day analysing the state of my mind for the last 53 years, but for me it is all quite logical. Having tried to repress the memory of this place for so long, yet lived with it every day, when I eventually came to talk about it, I simply had to return. Having done so, I certainly felt a shadow lifted, for both myself and the memory of Hutch.

Only one thing now remained for me to do and this was to meet Hjordis Spord, who so long ago had been our saviour. I was perturbed that whenever I had mentioned the Spords to our Norwegian hosts they seemed slightly embarrassed and would change the conversation. It was on the way back to Askvoll from Hindoy that Hoppy discovered that Olav Spord had been accused of collaborating with the Germans. This came as a shock to me and I immediately let it be known that without the Spords' help in providing food and dry clothing, I very much doubted that Hutch and I would have survived. Our hosts were unaware of the lengths the family had gone to to look after us, thinking only that they had informed on us. The Spords had contacted the police after our arrival in their house but I know that Olav Spord did so in an effort to help us and was unaware of the number of Quislings within the police who would report immediately to the Germans. Why would the family have treated us so well if they then meant to do us harm? As with many communities, memories are long, but I do hope that my protestations of the kindness we received at the hands of the Spords has helped to clear their name.

Before we returned to Bergen and the meeting with Hjordis, we enjoyed a day of celebrations with the people of Askvoll. I have rarely experienced such warmth and hospitality as we all received and I don't think any of us will forget such a wonderful place. I have certainly never heard such a heart-stirring rendering of 'Rule Britannia' as that which we were treated to at a concert in Askvoll church.

On Tuesday morning we bade our farewells to Askvoll and headed back to Bergen. We were met by Hjordis's son, Olav-Arne, who quite unexpectedly had arranged for some friends, Aud, Kate and Tor, to take us on a much-appreciated sightseeing visit before we went to his mother's house. I became very apprehensive as we neared the house and was most relieved when the rest of the party stayed in the garden talking, allowing me to go into the house alone. Walking into the sitting room I saw an old lady sitting in a chair, smiling in welcome. What else could I do but go up and hug and kiss her? For 53 years I had silently thanked her for saving me, and worried about her fate, now at last I could thank her properly. The tears poured down both our faces.

When the rest of the party came in, we sat down to a truly magnificent tea over which the talk never stopped. Being a very modest lady, Hjordis had told her son very little about her part in helping Hutch and myself, and he was most eager to hear the whole story.

I had always wanted to give Hjordis and her family a personal present. One of my wartime treasures were my original wings, presented to me at Shawbury FTS in September 1940. These were in very good condition as they were fixed to my 'best blue' uniform and had not suffered the rigours of sea water, yellow dye and life in a prisoner of war camp. A good friend, the late Bruce Bunning, was a gifted woodcarver and he had set the wings in a beautiful piece of walnut and inscribed a few words to the Spord family and the people of Askvoll. I had given this plaque to the Mayoress of

Askvoll who had decided it should sit in a prominent place in the town hall. Hjordis was only too happy to hear that this was where her present resided.

It seemed no time before Hoppy was reminding us that we had a flight to catch. The Tors insisted that they drive us to the airport, so having taken a fond leave of Hjordis we climbed into the waiting cars and headed for the airport.

I had done it. With the help of my fellow travellers, the people of Askvoll and a variety of people along the way, all of whom were indispensable, I had found and visited a tiny island which had haunted me for so many years. I felt an incredible elation as we left Norway, a feeling that lasted for some weeks after.

My one regret was that Hutch could not have been with me, but after my experiences at the drinking pool, I somehow felt that he hadn't been that far away. Many ragged memories were eased for me by this trip and in their place were memories of incredible friendship and kindness. All that remains for me to do is to say thank you from the bottom of my heart, to the people of Askvoll, for their hospitality on two occasions ... 53 years apart.

APPENDIX

Potato Farmer is Nazi Plane Crasher

When Flight-sergeant Martin Smith, aged 23, from his Beaufighter sighted a three-engined powerfully armed Blohm and Voss flying-boat in the North Sea, he raced in to attack.

His cannon shells crashed into the enemy and he saw the port wing catch fire. The flying-boat rolled over on its back and hit the sea, where it broke up and sank.

Smith whose home is at Thorney, Peterborough, was a potato farmer in civil life.

Now he belongs to a squadron of the keenest young men of Coastal Command, says Air Ministry News Service.

The squadron lives in a group of Nissen huts beside airfield runways in Scotland. The original members were mostly Londoners. Now it is almost an international brigade.

At his last station, in the South of England, Smith shot down two Heinkel 111s.

"Got Him Unawares"

His greatest friend is Sergeant Alan Welch, of Bromley, Kent, a 20-year-old pilot. Attacking a Heinkel 111 recently, Welch let fly with his cannon from dead astern. His aim was first-class that morning.

"I hit the starboard engine and undercarriage leg," he said. "The undercarriage came clean off, followed by bits of engine. I must have got him unawares. Anyway, he wallowed on for a bit, and then crashed into the sea.

"A few days later, though, one of his pals nearly got his own back on me. I met another Heinkel 111 and in the scrap that followed he hit my port wing and set it on fire.

"The navigator yelled to me to look, and I looked at the starboard wing. It was on fire, too. We throttled back and broke off the fight.

"I slipped to port, then to starboard, going as slowly as I could, and the flames went out. We got back to base all right."

Riddled With Holes

Squadron-leader Roger Morewood, aged 26, of Sunbury, Middlesex, said that once off the Zuider Zee he met five Messerschmitt 110s. He got away, though not before his airplane was riddled with cannon holes.

"The old bus let me down the other day, though," he said. "I was lucky enough to meet a Blohm and Voss flying-boat. I chased it, but the guns jammed right in the middle of my best burst. He must have realised that I had no guns, because he chucked everything at me before I could get away.

"Good old crates these, but I they only had another few knots in hand . . then we could really show them a ring or two."

One flight-commander is Squadron-leader David Cartridge, 23-year-old Bristolian. During the Vaagso Commando raid he shot down a Heinkel 111 and damaged a second. His formation shot down two out of a section of three.

Shot Up Airfield

Cartridge accompanied a formation of bombers which recently attacked Trondjeim. Finding things dull, he swooped down and shot up an airfield in the vicinity, then returned to the bombers.

The Squadron C.O., Wing-Commander R. Pike, is from Belfast. During the Coastal Command attack on the Prinz Eugen, he strafed a destroyer, silencing its fire. Companions on that exploit were Pilot-officer Jay (an American from Texas), and Pilot-officer Maurice, a Free Frenchman.

Evening Standard, 11 July 1942.

172

By the KING'S Order the name of
Flight Sergeant M. Smith,
Royal Air Force,
was published in the London Gazette on
11 June, 1942,
as mentioned in a Despatch for distinguished service.
I am charged to record
His Majesty's high appreciation.

Archibald Sinclair

Secretary of State for Air

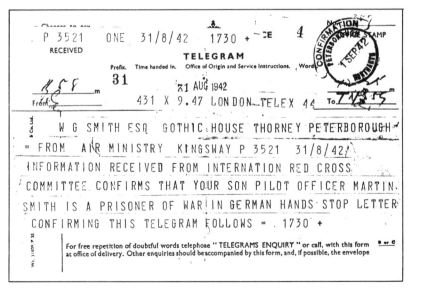

TELEPHONE   HOLBORN 3434.

Extn. 121.

Any communications on the
subject of this letter should
be addressed to :—
THE UNDER SECRETARY
OF STATE. AIR MINISTRY,
and the following number
quoted :—

A.M.3031/45/S.10a.

Your Ref. ....

AIR MINISTRY,

LONDON. W.C.2.

15th March, 1945.

Sir,

       I am directed to inform you that the King
has been graciously pleased to confer the
Distinguished Flying Medal on your son, Flight
Sergeant (now Flight Lieutenant) Martin SMITH with
effect from 20th July, 1942, for the services
detailed in the attached statement.   The award will
be published in the London Gazette (Royal Air Force
Awards Supplement) dated 20th March, 1945.

    2.   Arrangements will be made for your son
to attend an investiture on his return to this
country.

        I am, Sir,
           Your obedient Servant,

         H.F. Derbyshire

    W.G. Smith, Esq.,
       Gothic House,
         Thorney,
           Peterborough.

Distinguished Flying Medal

903053 Flight Sergeant Martin SMITH, No.248 Squadron.
This non-commissioned officer has shown great determination
and devotion to duty and carried out many attacks on
enemy shipping.   He made a reconnaissance along the
Norwegian coast, searching for the German naval vessel
Lutzow and he has attacked enemy shipping near Calais in
the face of heavy flak from the ships and from the shore
batteries.   Flight Sergeant Smith has destroyed 3 enemy
aircraft.

BUCKINGHAM PALACE.

I greatly regret that I am
unable to give you personally the
award which you have so well earned.

I now send it to you with
my congratulations and my best
wishes for your future happiness.

George R.I.

Flight Lieutenant Martin Smith, D.F.M.

175